The New York Times

IN THE HEADLINES

Assisted Suicide

IS IT RIGHT TO HAVE THE CHOICE?

THE NEW YORK TIMES EDITORIAL STAFF

Published in 2020 by New York Times Educational Publishing
in association with The Rosen Publishing Group, Inc.
29 East 21st Street, New York, NY 10010

First Edition

The New York Times
Alex Ward: Editorial Director, Book Development
Phyllis Collazo: Photo Rights/Permissions Editor
Heidi Giovine: Administrative Manager

Rosen Publishing
Megan Kellerman: Managing Editor
Julia Bosson: Editor
Greg Tucker: Creative Director
Brian Garvey: Art Director

Cataloging-in-Publication Data
Names: New York Times Company.
Title: Assisted suicide: is it right to have the choice? / edited by
the New York Times editorial staff.
Description: New York : New York Times Educational Publishing,
2020. | Series: In the headlines | Includes glossary and index.
Identifiers: ISBN 9781642822038 (library bound) | ISBN
9781642822021 (pbk.) | ISBN 9781642822045 (ebook)
Subjects: LCSH: Assisted suicide—Juvenile literature. | Assisted
suicide—Moral and ethical aspects—Juvenile literature. | Assisted
suicide—Social aspects—Juvenile literature.
Classification: LCC R726.A875 2020 | DDC 362.28—dc23

Manufactured in the United States of America

On the cover: Illustration by Hokyoung Kim.

Contents

CHAPTER 2

Ethical, Legal and Political Issues

CHAPTER 5

Reaching the End

Introduction

ON NOV. 1, 2014, Brittany Maynard took a mixture of barbiturates, ending her own life with her family by her side. Her death received national attention: After her diagnosis of terminal brain cancer at the age of 29, Maynard became a vocal supporter of the Death With Dignity movement, advocating for the right of individuals to have choice in the ending of their lives. A letter she wrote outlining her circumstances and her beliefs for CNN went viral, drawing attention to the issue of assisted suicide.

Maynard's death became a turning point for the debate of assisted suicide (although many proponents prefer the term "aid in dying"). Supporters of the movement were galvanized by her articulate plea for the autonomy to end her own life, while detractors worried about the ethics of ending someone's life and the precedent that would establish. Following her death, California became the fifth state to legalize physician-assisted suicide.

Assisted suicide might be one of the most polarizing issues Americans face today. Brought into view by the practices of Dr. Jack Kevorkian, who in the 1990s illegally assisted hundreds of patients in ending their own lives, America's understanding of assisted suicide has evolved over the years. Today, with more and more states voting on measures to expand the availability of physician-assisted suicide to terminally ill and elderly individuals, the legality and acceptability of the practice seems to be increasing.

And yet, views on the issue vary greatly. Those with the widest range of views are doctors, who might routinely see patients suffer from long illnesses, but who are also bound to follow the Hippocratic oath to do no harm. Religious groups see little distinction between euthanasia

John Shields with his wife, Robin June Hood, and their dog Diego in Victoria, British Columbia on March 15, 2017. The Canadian government legalized what it termed "medical assistance in dying," which allowed patients like Shields to feel empowered over his incurable disease rather than feel crippled by it.

and murder. Men and women who have seen family members die prolonged painful deaths advocate passionately for the right to choose, seeing the possibility for shortening an unbeatable agony. And individuals with chronic and long-term illnesses are split: While many fight for the possibility of choice, others are wary of measures that might give someone else the authority to end their lives without their full consent.

The debate over assisted suicide bridges a number of ethical dilemmas. If parties can agree that terminally ill individuals can have the right to end their lives, then the question becomes: What determines a terminal illness? Should elderly adults who are suffering from no acute symptoms but whose quality of life has deteriorated also be eligible for assisted suicide? In other words, where do we draw the line?

Even as America struggles to identify the solutions to these questions, internationally, assisted suicide has expanded throughout Europe. The Netherlands is a pioneer in the administration of physician-assisted suicide, allowing for anyone with "unbearable suffering" to make the choice to end their own lives. In Italy, a few recent cases have divided the public and resulted in new laws that allow for refusal of end-of-life care, and in France, legal challenges are still making their way through the system.

The articles in this book speak to the array of ethical quandaries, legal battles and personal stories that make up the face of this uniquely complicated issue. They speak to what's at stake for individuals who have requested the right to die as well as to what makes fulfilling their desires so challenging. The reporting covers the history of the Dying With Dignity movement in all its incarnations, from its grassroots origins to its increasing legal acceptance.

The last chapter of this book is devoted to a single story published by The New York Times in 2017. Reported by Catherine Porter, the story follows John Shields, a retired chaplain in Vancouver who decided to arrange and hold his own wake before ending his life. What emerges from this story is a testament to the personal significance of assisted suicide for individuals and their loved ones.

CHAPTER 1

Making the Case for Assisted Suicide

The issue of assisted suicide brings up a vast array of moral and ethical dilemmas individually and collectively. And yet it has also gained a devoted group of advocates who passionately make the case for its legality. In this chapter, writers, doctors, family members and terminally ill individuals measure what is at stake in end-of-life care, arguing for why physician-assisted suicide might be necessary and examining when it might result in unintended consequences.

Fatal Mercies

OPINION | BY FRANK BRUNI | AUG. 10, 2013

FEW OF US get anything approaching the degree of control we'd like over our lives. Must we also be denied a reasonable measure over our deaths?

That's all that Joseph Yourshaw, 93, seemingly wanted: to exit on his own terms, at home, without growing any weaker, without suffering any more. And that's all that one of his daughters, Barbara Mancini, 57, was trying to help him do, according to the police report that set her criminal prosecution in motion.

She's charged, under Pennsylvania law, with aiding a suicide, a felony punishable by up to 10 years in prison. Such a sentence would be ludicrous, but so, by all appearances, is the case against her: a waste of public resources, a needless infliction of pain on a family already grieving, and a senseless prioritization of a frequently ignored (and easily ignorable) law over logic, compassion, decency.

It would have been easy for prosecutors to walk away; that sort of thing happens all the time. That it didn't happen here suggests how conflicted, inconsistent and bullheaded we Americans can be when it comes to the very private, very intimate business of dying.

These are the facts of the case, according to public records and news reports:

Yourshaw was receiving hospice care at his home in the small central Pennsylvania city of Pottsville. A decorated World War II veteran who had gone on to run his own contracting business, he was terminally ill, with severe diabetes, heart disease and kidney disease, among other ailments. He was frail and in pain, and had indicated a yearning for an end to it all.

On Feb. 7, he sought one, swallowing an unusually large measure of his morphine in the presence of Mancini, who did nothing about it. A hospice nurse who stopped by the house afterward found him unresponsive and later said that Mancini, herself a nurse, confessed to having provided him, at his request, a vial or bottle of his painkiller that contained a potentially lethal dose.

The hospice nurse called 911. The police and paramedics arrived. Although Mancini insisted that her father did not want to be revived, he was given medical attention and brought to a local hospital, where his condition stabilized. He nonetheless died there on Feb. 11. He did not get to spend his final days in his own home or his final hours in his own bed.

The statement of the police officer who interacted with Mancini on the day of the overdose says, "She told me that her father had asked her for all his morphine so he could commit suicide, and she provided it." Mancini, through her lawyers, later denied that she was deliberately enabling him to end his life. Trying to reconcile these conflicting claims is, for now, impossible: a judge has issued a gag order for the main players in the case, which is headed to trial, barring a plea agreement or a prosecutorial change of heart.

But nowhere can I find any dispute that Mancini's 93-year-old father was fading and hurting. Nowhere can I find any insinuation that Mancini coaxed him toward suicide. Or poured the morphine down his throat. Or did anything more than hand it to him. That's it.

And the lightness of this alleged assist, coupled with the ambiguity of its connection to his death after he'd rebounded from the overdose, has not only provoked outrage from Compassion and Choices, an organization that supports more options in end-of-life care.

It has also prompted befuddlement on the other side of the issue, with a leading opponent of assisted suicide scratching his head about the way the case is being handled. "It is odd to see one like this prosecuted," Stephen Drake, the research analyst for the advocacy group Not Dead Yet, told me.

He added that the case worries him, because if it gets significant publicity and informs what many people believe assisted suicide is, they'll see it as a more benign act than he believes they should. "It's going to make it even harder to prosecute ones that really call out to be prosecuted," he said.

Such prosecutions are rare all in all, even though assisted suicide — under medical supervision and specific circumstances — is legal in only four states: Oregon, Washington, Montana and, as of a few months ago, Vermont.

Alan Meisel, the founder and director of the Center for Bioethics and Health Law at the University of Pittsburgh, said that that's partly because "these kinds of things usually happen in secret."

But that's also because when they do come to light, the police and prosecutors exercise enormous discretion, knowing that there are all kinds of gray areas in which the law is a clumsy, crude instrument; that a jury may be loath to punish a gesture of apparent mercy; and that it's not uncommon for death to be hastened by painkillers, even in hospitals.

Did Mancini break the law? If the accounts of both the hospice nurse and the police officer are accurate, probably so, but the Pennsylvania statute that forbids assisted suicide, like similar statutes in other states, is worded broadly and says nothing about what rises to the level of assistance.

That vagueness can be a blessing, allowing the police and prosecutors to filter the law through their own good judgment and sensitivity. No such filter has been applied here, at least based on the evidence presented at a preliminary court hearing early this month.

A spokesman for the Pennsylvania attorney general's office, which is in charge of the prosecution, declined to comment for this column, citing the gag order. So I couldn't ask anyone there how, in an era of severely limited government resources, the dedication of time and money to this case made any sense.

I couldn't ask anyone how, precisely, Mancini had done her father wrong. I couldn't point out that his widow — her mother — had spoken out in defense of her before everyone involved stopped talking. I couldn't note the different exit made recently by a terminally ill journalist in Seattle, thanks to Washington's Death With Dignity Act.

Her name was Jane Lotter, and last week, in The Times, Michael Winerip wrote this of her last moments with her family, including her husband, Bob Marts:

"On July 18, the couple and their two children gathered in the parents' bedroom. Ms. Lotter asked to keep in her contact lenses, in case a hummingbird came to the feeder Mr. Marts had hung outside their window. The last song she heard before pouring powdered barbiturates, provided by hospice officials, into a glass of grape juice was George Gershwin's 'Lullaby.' Then she hugged and kissed them all goodbye, swallowed the drink and, within minutes, lapsed into a coma and died."

No paramedics. No arrest. No need.

FRANK BRUNI is an Op-Ed columnist for The New York Times.

For Those at Death's Door, a Case for 'Life Panels'

ESSAY | BY BOB GOLDMAN | NOV. 19, 2013

AT THE BEGINNING of 2012, my mother was 95 years old. She lived in an assisted-living center, with hospice care, in a hospital bed 24/7. She was hollow-eyed and emaciated. Though she had moments of clarity, she was confused, anxious and uncomfortable. Her quality of life was minimal, at best. And the cost to keep her in this condition had risen to close to $100,000 a year.

Three years earlier, when she was completely rational, my mother told me that while she had lived a full and rewarding life, she was ready to go. By 2012, when her life was more punishment than reward, she did not have the mental faculties to reaffirm her desire, nor was there a legal way to carry out her decision. Even if my mother had been living in one of the states like Oregon, Washington or Vermont that have "death with dignity" statutes on their books, the fact that she lacked mental competency to request an assisted death by 2012 almost certainly would have ruled out any possibility that the state would have granted her wish.

Nor would it have been an option to move her to one of the few countries that have removed the legal perils of a decision to end one's life. It was hard enough to get my mother from her bed to her chair. How would I have transported her to the Netherlands?

No, there is only one solution to this type of situation, for anyone who may encounter it in the future. What is needed here, I suggest, is not a death panel. It's a "life panel" with the legal authority to ensure that my mother's request to end her own life, on her own terms, would be honored.

I am staking a claim on the name life panel, because the concept of death panels has been so irresponsibly bandied about during debates about the government's involvement in health care. But I really do not

FEDERICA BORDONI

want to discuss politics here. I am a financial planner, and I want to focus on money.

The financial aspects of the end of life are an integral part of almost every plan I create. If planning is about getting from Point A to Point B, you do not get a bigger or more definitive Point B than your own funeral.

Some of my clients are extremely realistic about the crushing expenses they could face in their final years. Others are more sanguine. When I tell them that their money is unlikely to last through their 90s, they say: "Well, that's O.K. I don't plan to live past 85, anyway." I have a standard answer in these cases. I say: "Yes, you expect to die at 85, but what if you're unlucky? What if you live to 95?" At that point, I tell them about my mother. Then we get down to work.

Occasionally, people tell me that their end dates are guaranteed. They are saving pills that will put them out of their misery, or they have made "arrangements" with friends. For all their planning, my clients do not realize that when the time comes, they may be too sick or demented to carry out their do-it-yourself strategies. And so we come back to the life panel. Who is on it? Certainly, a doctor would be involved. After all, we laymen might feel guilty about making decisions that would hasten the end of a life, but under current law in most states, doctors would be guilty — of murder. On a life panel, a doctor would be held blameless. And I would have no problem adding a medical ethicist and a therapist.

Most important, I think the individual should be allowed to nominate panelists who are likely to understand the person's wishes: family members, close friends, a person with whom they share religious beliefs.

This may seem like a reach, but in fact we already come quite close to this now. As any financial planner will tell you, everyone needs a living will. This is a legal document that instructs a surrogate or a medical center on the level of life-prolonging or palliative care you want if you become unable to make medical decisions.

But legal documents go only so far. Doctors I have asked about this issue know firsthand the uncertainties of deciding when a person has lost medical decision-making capacity. Nor is it possible to write out instructions for every possible medical eventuality.

A life panel might not be the perfect solution, but neither is draining a family's resources to support a joyless existence in a hospital bed.

Those who understand the high cost of quality care often compliment me on what a good son I am to pay so much for my mother for so long. The truth is, it was her money. But it was my money, and my children's money as well, at least according to my mother. My parents did not want to "die with just a dollar." They worked hard behind the counter of a small retail store to leave money to their children. It was of primary importance to them, as it is to many of my clients.

So what should have been done for my mother?

Three years before, deciding to convene a life panel was a choice she could have made herself. I can almost see the members of the panel squeezed into her studio apartment as she informed them, as she frequently informed me, that while she had enjoyed a wonderful life, "enough was enough."

The panel might have rejected this appeal, as I did many times over the years. They would have checked her medications, scheduled her with a geriatric psychiatrist and suggested that she return to the wheelchair bocce team that had won the championship at her assisted living center. At the end of the meeting, they would have promised to review her case regularly, to see if her mind — or her body — had changed.

In the years that followed, it would have been up to me, as her surrogate, to keep the life panel informed. If and when the panel did agree that the quality of her life was not what she would have wanted to preserve, it could have ordered a prescription for intravenous morphine for her doctor to administer. Or, in do-it-yourself mode, we could have used a fentanyl patch. Either drug in higher-than-therapeutic doses is painless and very effective.

Instead of the uncertainty that leaves so many people racing back and forth across the country to be at the deathbed of a loved one, my mother's end would have been scheduled, so family and friends would be sure to be present. There would have been grief, but not, I think, a lot of regret. The life panel would not have made an arbitrary decision to end my mother's life. This would not have been a judgment based on societal or governmental standards. The panel would have simply, and thoughtfully, carried out my mother's wishes.

Does all of this sound gloomy? I'm not sure. Is it worth whatever money it costs to keep everyone alive as long as possible, no matter how terrible their lives may be? I don't know. What I do know is that the expense of prolonging our lives can be devastating. There has to be a better way.

As for my mother, convening a life panel is no longer a possibility. She died later in 2012. Thanks largely to hospice care in her final days, it was a relatively easy passing from my point of view and certainly a lot less painful than the months and years before had been. That is why I still think it should have happened at least three years earlier.

A life panel might not have agreed, but at least the issues would be aired.

With a life panel, we could have ensured a timely and respectful end. But with society unprepared to face the reality of death, there could have been one other solution for my mother, one that is still available for many others like her. On one of my visits, I could have put on my financial planner hat and told my mother exactly how much her end-of-life care was costing. Because I was handling her affairs, she never knew the price tag.

I'm sure she would not have believed it, and I doubt she would have survived it.

BOB GOLDMAN is a financial planner in Sausalito, Calif.

Weighing the End of Life

OPINION | BY LOUISE ARONSON | FEB. 2, 2013

ONE WEEKEND LAST YEAR, we asked our vet how we would know when it was time to put down Byron, our elderly dog. Byron was 14, half blind, partly deaf, with dementia, arthritis and an enlarged prostate. He often walked into walls, stood staring vacantly with his tail down, and had begun wandering and whining for reasons we could not always decipher.

Attentive to Byron's needs, we softened his food with water and sprinkled it with meat; we cuddled him when he whimpered and took him outside to relieve himself seven, even eight times a night. We couldn't take a vacation because we couldn't imagine asking anyone, friend or dog sitter, to do what we were doing. Nor could we fully trust anyone to provide the care we thought Byron required.

But it was also true that Byron often toddled along happily on his daily walks. He sniffed bushes and stained storefronts with the measured attentiveness of a research scientist, flirted with passers-by, and on occasion raised his ears and tail, marked a spot, then kicked his hind legs while growling, barking and asserting his dominance over some generally long-gone canine competition. Since Byron was an evidently elderly eight-pound Yorkshire terrier, this invariably provoked fond smiles from passing strangers.

When asked whether it was time to put Byron "to sleep," our vet said he used the 50 percent rule: Were at least half of Byron's days good days? Or was it two bad days for every good? When you get to the latter, he explained, it's time.

This conversation gave me pause for two reasons. First, what did Byron want? Was 50 percent good enough for him? How about 70? Or 20? There was, of course, no way to know.

Which brings me to my second reason for pause. When not serving as faithful servant to our tiny dog, I am a geriatrician. Because older adults have a greater range of needs and abilities than any other age group, and because there is a national shortage of geriatricians, I care for the frailest and sickest among them.

To many people's surprise, most of my patients are as satisfied with their lives as they were when they were less debilitated. But this isn't true for everyone, and some are eager to say they've had enough. They are bedbound or dependent, unable to do any of the things they once valued so dearly — working, caring for their families, eating solid food or even hearing the conversation of those who come to see them. Still others cannot express their wishes or needs but sit propped in chairs frowning and grimacing, despite attentive care and trials of antidepressants and pain medications.

"Why doesn't God want me?" asked a 96-year-old felled by multiple strokes and fed through a tube.

"Can't you do something?" begged an 89-year-old with advanced Parkinson's disease and incontinence who would have killed himself if only he still could.

LAURA CARLIN

And these were two people who lived relatively comfortably with frequent visits from loving families. But others, even those with similar or equal disabilities, might feel just as strongly that they want to preserve their lives at any cost. They would never choose euthanasia.

Of course, we can't have a 50 percent rule for humans. Because who decides? These are vulnerable people, and while the world is full of dedicated, self-sacrificing caregivers, it also contains far too many people who stand to gain from death (through inheritance) or from continuing life (in the form of Social Security checks or cheap housing).

For Byron, the fateful day came both slowly and suddenly. Over his last year, he'd had a number of health problems, and we had intended to take a palliative approach: doing only those treatments that lessened his suffering and avoiding tests and stressful vet visits at all costs. But then his paw hurt, so we took him in. He didn't respond to the first antibiotic so sedation and a biopsy were required. Next, he developed bloody, watery stool. We talked the vet into prescribing standard antibiotics without a visit, and he improved. But a few months later, he was short of breath. He needed an X-ray to determine that it was pneumonia, then oxygen and more antibiotics. He stayed overnight. A few months after that, pus dripped from his red, swollen eyes — conjunctivitis. Each time he had to go to the vet, he shook, panted, climbed up our bodies, and tugged on his leash, his tiny body straining for the door.

Suddenly, I fully understood something I observed at work all the time — how it was possible to love a frail relative, prioritize his comfort and well-being, and yet repeatedly find oneself doing things that felt awful to everyone.

Finally we made an appointment with a hospice vet. When I returned home from work that night, the humans of our family were cradling Byron and looking sad. He ran to me, wiggling his tail. He hadn't eaten all day. I thawed some chicken, and he gobbled it down. Someone said, "You can't kill him."

Then he followed me to the bathroom and vomited the chicken onto the floor at my feet. He stood, tail down, facing the wall.

That night, the vet gave him the injection, and Byron died in our arms.

Since then, I have often wondered whether we waited too long. We counted the time he spent sleeping as contentment, tipping the scale above the 50 percent mark. But I know that in elderly humans, sleep is more often a sign of chronic exhaustion, depression and avoidance of pain. In dealing with the guilt brought on by our mixed feelings — we love him; he's ruining our lives — I realize we may have overcompensated to his detriment.

With dying humans, similar situations arise every day: hospital stays that fix the acute problem and worsen the chronic ones; emergency department visits that yield diagnoses but require weeks of recovery from the waiting and testing; surgeries that are themselves minor but provoke major confusion, complications and hated nursing home stays. On the other hand, there are the relatively simple problems that might be addressed by a doctor if only seeing one didn't require an ambulance for transportation, or time off work by an adult child, or more taxi fare than remains in the Social Security check, or more effort than seems worth the while.

And sometimes it's even more complicated than that. Last year, a patient of mine with 15 major medical problems, including a form of leukemia, decided he didn't ever want to return to the hospital, do chemotherapy, or try any of the other treatments we discussed. But for weeks after that, he railed and fumed at the prospect of palliative care, because he wanted very badly to live.

He wanted to live — just not in the hospital, with poisons in his blood. He was sick and tired of feeling sick and tired. Like so many, his was a reasoned and reasonable stance.

LOUISE ARONSON is an associate professor of medicine at the University of California, San Francisco, and the author of "A History of the Present Illness."

Suicide by Choice? Not So Fast

OPINION | BY BEN MATTLIN | OCT. 31, 2012

NEXT WEEK, VOTERS in Massachusetts will decide whether to adopt an assisted-suicide law. As a good pro-choice liberal, I ought to support the effort. But as a lifelong disabled person, I cannot.

There are solid arguments in favor. No one will be coerced into taking a poison pill, supporters insist. The "right to die" will apply only to those with six months to live or less. Doctors will take into account the possibility of depression. There is no slippery slope.

Fair enough, but I remain skeptical. There's been scant evidence of abuse so far in Oregon, Washington and Montana, the three states where physician-assisted death is already legal, but abuse — whether spousal, child or elder — is notoriously underreported, and evidence is difficult to come by. What's more, Massachusetts registered nearly 20,000 cases of elder abuse in 2010 alone.

My problem, ultimately, is this: I've lived so close to death for so long that I know how thin and porous the border between coercion and free choice is, how easy it is for someone to inadvertently influence you to feel devalued and hopeless — to pressure you ever so slightly but decidedly into being "reasonable," to unburdening others, to "letting go."

Perhaps, as advocates contend, you can't understand why anyone would push for assisted-suicide legislation until you've seen a loved one suffer. But you also can't truly conceive of the many subtle forces — invariably well meaning, kindhearted, even gentle, yet as persuasive as a tsunami — that emerge when your physical autonomy is hopelessly compromised.

I was born with a congenital neuromuscular weakness called spinal muscular atrophy. I've never walked or stood or had much use of my hands. Roughly half the babies who exhibit symptoms as I did don't live past age 2. Not only did I survive, but the progression of my disease

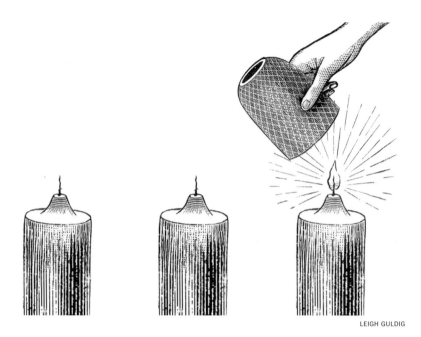

LEIGH GULDIG

slowed dramatically when I was about 6 years old, astounding doctors. Today, at nearly 50, I'm a husband, father, journalist and author.

Yet I'm more fragile now than I was in infancy. No longer able to hold a pencil, I'm writing this with a voice-controlled computer. Every swallow of food, sometimes every breath, can become a battle. And a few years ago, when a surgical blunder put me into a coma from septic shock, the doctors seriously questioned whether it was worth trying to extend my life. My existence seemed pretty tenuous anyway, they figured. They didn't know about my family, my career, my aspirations.

Fortunately, they asked my wife, who knows exactly how I feel. She convinced them to proceed "full code," as she's learned to say, to keep me alive using any and all means necessary.

From this I learned how easy it is to be perceived as someone whose quality of life is untenable, even or perhaps especially by doctors. Indeed, I hear it from them all the time — "How have you survived so long? Wow, you must put up with a lot!" — even during routine office visits, when all I've asked for is an antibiotic for a sinus infection. Strangers don't treat me this way, but doctors feel entitled to render judgments and voice their opinions. To them, I suppose, I must represent a failure of their profession, which is shortsighted. I am more than my diagnosis and my prognosis.

This is but one of many invisible forces of coercion. Others include that certain look of exhaustion in a loved one's eyes, or the way nurses and friends sigh in your presence while you're zoned out in a hospital bed. All these can cast a dangerous cloud of depression upon even the most cheery of optimists, a situation clinicians might misread since, to them, it seems perfectly rational.

And in a sense, it is rational, given the dearth of alternatives. If nobody wants you at the party, why should you stay? Advocates of Death With Dignity laws who say that patients themselves should decide whether to live or die are fantasizing. Who chooses suicide in a vacuum? We are inexorably affected by our immediate environment. The deck is stacked.

Yes, that may sound paranoid. After all, the Massachusetts proposal calls for the lethal dose to be "self-administered," which it defines as the "patient's act of ingesting." You might wonder how that would apply to those who can't feed themselves — people like me. But as I understand the legislation, there is nothing to prevent the patient from designating just about anyone to feed them the poison pill. Indeed, there is no requirement for oversight of the ingestion at all; no one has to witness how and when the lethal drug is given. Which, to my mind, leaves even more room for abuse.

To be sure, there are noble intentions behind the "assisted death" proposals, but I can't help wondering why we're in such a hurry to ensure the right to die before we've done all we can to ensure that those of us with severe, untreatable, life-threatening conditions are given the same open-hearted welcome, the same open-minded respect and the same open-ended opportunities due everyone else.

BEN MATTLIN is a freelance journalist and the author of "Miracle Boy Grows Up: How the Disability Rights Revolution Saved My Sanity."

The Last Right

OPINION | BY ROSS DOUTHAT | OCT. 11, 2014

ON NOV. 1, barring the medically unexpected or a change of heart, a young woman named Brittany Maynard will ingest a lethal prescription and die by suicide.

Maynard is 29, recently married and is suffering from terminal brain cancer. After deciding against hospice care — fearing, she wrote in a CNN op-ed, a combination of pain, personality changes, and the loss of basic mental and physical functions — she and her husband moved from California to Oregon, one of five states that permit physician-assisted suicide. In the time remaining to her, she has become a public advocate for that practice's expansion, recording testimonials on behalf of the right of the terminally ill to make their quietus.

The tragedy here is almost deep enough to drown the political debate. But that debate's continued existence is still a striking fact. Why, in a society where individualism seems to be carrying the day, is the right that Maynard intends to exercise still confined to just a handful of states? Why has assisted suicide's advance been slow, when on other social issues the landscape has shifted dramatically in a libertarian direction?

Twenty years ago, a much more rapid advance seemed likely. Some sort of right to suicide seemed like a potential extension of "the right to define one's own concept of existence" that the Supreme Court had invoked while upholding a woman's constitutional right to abortion. Polls in the 1990s consistently showed more support — majority support, depending on the framing — for physician-assisted suicide than for what then seemed like the eccentric cause of same-sex marriage.

Yet the latter cause has triumphed sweepingly, while voluntary euthanasia has advanced only haltingly. Part of the explanation lies with the Supreme Court, which in 1997 ruled 9 to 0 that the Constitution does not include a right to suicide. But the court would not have ruled as it did absent a deeper reality: Many liberals seem considerably more uncomfortable with the idea of physician-assisted suicide than with other causes, from abortion to homosexuality, where claims about personal autonomy and liberty are at stake.

Conservatives oppose assisted suicide more fiercely, but it's a persistent left-of-center discomfort, even among the most secular liberals, that's really held the idea at bay. Indeed, on this issue you can find many liberal writers who sound like, well, social conservatives — who warn of the danger of a lives-not-worth-living mentality, acknowledge the ease with which ethical and legal slopes can slip, recognize the limits of "consent" alone as a standard for moral judgment.

At the same time, though, there are tensions within the liberal mind on this issue, particularly when the discussion moves from the general (why assisted suicide is unwise as public policy) to the particular (why life is still worth living after all hope is lost, and why a given person facing death shouldn't avail themselves of suicide).

You can see that tension illustrated, in a fascinating way, in the work of Ezekiel Emanuel, the health care expert and bioethicist (and brother of Chicago's mayor). Emanuel's 1997 Atlantic essay on physician-assisted suicide remains the best liberal critique of the idea, and he reiterated his anti-suicide position this fall, again in the Atlantic, in an essay discussing his perspective on aging, medicine and death.

But the new essay — which ran under the headline "Why I Hope to Die at 75" — was also shot through with precisely the fear of diminishment and incapacity, the anxiety at being any kind of burden, the desire to somehow exit at one's sharpest and fittest and best, that drives the impulse toward medicalized suicide. It was partially a powerful case against unnecessary medical treatment — but partially a window into a worldview ill equipped to make sense of suffering that's bound to lead to death, or that does not have a mountain-climbing, op-ed-writing recovery at the end of it.

The same deficit is apparent in responses to Brittany Maynard's plight. Liberal policy writers are comfortable using her case to discuss the inadequacies of end-of-life care (as the health care expert Harold Pollack did, eloquently, in a piece for The New Republic). But when it comes time to make an affirmative case for what she actually has to live for, they often demur. To find that case, you often have to turn to explicitly religious writers — like Kara Tippetts, a mother of four currently dying of her own cancer, who wrote Maynard a passionate open letter urging her to embrace the possibility that their shared trial could actually have a purpose, that "beauty will meet us in that last breath."

The future of the assisted suicide debate may depend, in part, on whether Tippetts's case for the worth of what can seem like pointless suffering can be made either without her theological perspective, or by a liberalism more open to metaphysical arguments than the left is today.

If it can, then laws like Oregon's will remain unusual, and the politics of assisted suicide the exception to the ever-more-libertarian trend.

If it can't, then many more tragic stories will have the ending Brittany Maynard has chosen to embrace.

ROSS DOUTHAT is an Op-Ed columnist for The New York Times.

On Assisted Suicide, Going Beyond 'Do No Harm'

OPINION | BY HAIDER JAVED WARRAICH | NOV. 4, 2016

DURHAM, N.C. — Out of nowhere, a patient I recently met in my clinic told me, "If my heart stops, doctor, just let me go."

"Why?" I asked him.

Without hesitating, he replied, "Because there are worse states than death."

Advances in medical therapies, in addition to their immense benefits, have changed death to dying — from an instantaneous event to a long, drawn-out process. Death is preceded by years of disability, countless procedures and powerful medications. Only one in five patients is able to die at home. These days many patients fear what it takes to live more than death itself.

That may explain why this year, behind the noise of the presidential campaign, the right-to-die movement has made several big legislative advances. In June, California became the fifth and largest state to put an assisted suicide law into effect; this week the District of Columbia Council passed a similar law. And on Tuesday voters in Colorado will decide whether to allow physician-assisted suicide in their state as well.

Yet even as assisted suicide has generated broader support, the group most vehemently opposed to it hasn't budged: doctors.

That resistance is traditionally couched in doctors' adherence to our understanding of the Hippocratic oath. But it's becoming harder for us to know what is meant by "do no harm." With the amount of respirators and other apparatus at our disposal, it is almost impossible for most patients to die unless doctors' or patients' families end life support. The withdrawal of treatment, therefore, is now perhaps the most common way critically ill patients die in the hospital.

While "withdrawal" implies a passive act, terminating artificial support feels decidedly active. Unlike assisted suicide, which requires patients to be screened for depression, patients can ask for treatment withdrawal even if they have major depression or are suicidal. Furthermore, withdrawal decisions are usually made for patients who are so sick that they frequently have no voice in the matter.

Some doctors skirt the question of assisted suicide through opiate prescriptions, which are almost universally prescribed for patients nearing death. Even though these medications can slow down breathing to the point of stoppage, doctors and nurses are very comfortable giving them, knowing that they might hasten a "natural" death.

In extreme cases, when even morphine isn't enough, patients are given anesthesia to ease their deaths. The last time I administered what is called terminal sedation, another accepted strategy, was in the case of a patient with abdominal cancer whose intestines were perforated and for whom surgery was not an option. The patient, who had been writhing uncontrollably in pain, was finally comfortable. Yet terminal sedation, necessary as it was, felt closer to active euthanasia than assisted suicide would have.

While the way people die has changed, the arguments made against assisted suicide have not. We are warned of a slippery slope, implying that legalization of assisted suicide would eventually lead to eugenic sterilization reminiscent of Nazi Germany. But no such drift has been observed in any of the countries where it has been legalized.

We are cautioned that legalization would put vulnerable populations like the uninsured and the disabled at risk; however, years of data from Oregon demonstrate that the vast majority of patients who opt for it are white, affluent and highly educated.

We are also told that assisted suicide laws will allow doctors and nurses to avoid providing high-quality palliative care to patients, but the data suggests the opposite: A strong argument for legalization is that it sensitizes doctors about ensuring the comfort of patients with terminal illnesses; if suicide is an option, they'll do what they can to preclude it.

And, again, we are counseled that physicians should do no harm. But medical harm is already one of the leading causes of death — and in any case, isn't preventing patients from dying on their terms its own form of medical harm?

With the right safeguards in place, assisted suicide can help give terminally ill patients a semblance of control over their lives as disease, disability and the medical machine tries to wrest it away from them. In Oregon, of the exceedingly few patients who have requested a lethal prescription — 1,545 in 18 years — about 35 percent never uses it; for them, it is merely a means to self-affirmation, a reassuring option.

Instead of using our energies to obfuscate and obstruct how patients might want to end their lives when faced with life-limiting disease, we physicians need to reassess how we can help patients achieve their goals when the end is near. We need to be able to offer an option for those who desire assisted suicide, so that they can openly take control of their death.

Instead of seeking guidance from ancient edicts, we need to reevaluate just what patients face in modern times. Even if it is a course we personally wouldn't recommend, we should consider allowing it for patients suffering from debilitating disease. How we die has changed tremendously over the past few decades — and so must we.

HAIDER JAVED WARRAICH, a fellow in cardiovascular medicine at Duke University Medical Center, is the author of the forthcoming book "Modern Death: How Medicine Changed the End of Life."

Should I Help My Patients Die?

OPINION | BY JESSICA NUTIK ZITTER | AUG. 5, 2017

OAKLAND, CALIF. — I was leafing through a patient's chart last year when a colleague tapped me on the shoulder. "I have a patient who is asking about the End of Life Option Act," he said in a low voice. "Can we even do that here?"

I practice both critical and palliative care medicine at a public hospital in Oakland. In June 2016, our state became the fourth in the nation to allow medical aid in dying for patients suffering from terminal illness. Oregon was the pioneer 20 years ago. Washington and Vermont followed suit more recently. (Colorado voters passed a similar law in November.) Now, five months after the law took effect here in California, I was facing my first request for assistance to shorten the life of a patient.

That week, I was the attending physician on the palliative care service. Since palliative care medicine focuses on the treatment of all forms of suffering in serious illness, my colleague assumed that I would know what to do with this request. I didn't.

I could see my own discomfort mirrored in his face. "Can you help us with it?" he asked me. "Of course," I said. Then I felt my stomach lurch.

California's law permits physicians to prescribe a lethal cocktail to patients who request it and meet certain criteria: They must be adults expected to die within six months who are able to self-administer the drug and retain the mental capacity to make a decision like this.

But that is where the law leaves off. The details of patient selection and protocol, even the composition of the lethal compound, are left to the individual doctor or hospital policy. Our hospital, like many others at that time, was still in the early stages of creating a policy and procedure. To me and many of my colleagues in California, it felt as if the law had passed so quickly that we weren't fully prepared to deal with it.

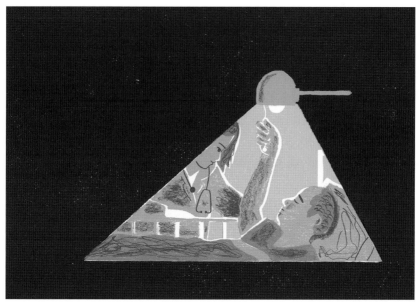

That aside, the idea of hastening death is uncomfortable for many doctors. In its original version, the Hippocratic oath states, "I will not administer poison to anyone when asked to do so, nor suggest such a course." The American Medical Association, the nation's largest association of doctors, has been formally opposed to the practice for 23 years. Its ethical and judicial council has recently begun to study the issue further.

At a dinner shortly after the law went into effect, I polled 10 palliative care colleagues on their impressions of it. There was a chorus of groans. Like me, they were being asked about it with increasing frequency, yet hadn't found an answer that felt right. It wasn't necessarily that we disapproved, but we didn't want to automatically become the go-to people on this very complex issue, either.

This first patient of mine was not a simple case. When I walked into his room, he glared at me. "Are you here to help me with this aid-in-dying thing?" he asked. He was in his early 60s, thin and tired, but in no obvious distress. From my read of his chart, he met all criteria to qualify. Terminal illness, decision-making capacity, ability to self-administer the medications. And he had made the requisite first request for the drugs two weeks earlier, as procedure dictates.

When I asked why he wanted to end his life early, he shrugged. "I'm just sick of living." I asked about any symptoms that might lie behind his request: unrelenting pain, nausea, shortness of breath. He denied them all. In palliative care, we are taught that suffering can take many forms besides the physical. I probed further and the floodgates opened.

He felt abandoned by his sister. She cared only about his Social Security payments, he said, and had gone AWOL now that the checks were being mailed to her house. Their love-hate relationship spanned decades, and they were now on the outs. His despair had given way to rage.

"Let's just end this," he said. "I'm fed up with my lousy life." He really didn't care, he added, that his sister opposed his decision.

His request appeared to stem from a deep family wound, not his terminal illness. I felt he wanted to punish his sister, and he had found a way to do it.

At our second meeting, with more trust established, he issued a sob, almost a keening. He felt terrified and powerless, he said. He didn't want to live this way anymore.

I understood. I could imagine my own distress in his condition — being shuttled like a bag of bones between the nursing home and the hospital. It was his legal right to request this intervention from me. But given how uncomfortable I was feeling, was it my right to say no?

In the end, he gave me an out. He agreed to a trial of antidepressants. "I'll give you four weeks," he said. He would follow up with his primary care doctor. I couldn't help feeling relieved.

The patient died in a nursing home, of natural causes, three months later. And I haven't had another request since. But the case left me worried. What if he had insisted on going through with it?

I'll admit it: I want this option available to me and my family. I have seen much suffering around death. In my experience, most of the pain can be managed by expert care teams focusing on symptom management and family support. But not all. My mother is profoundly claustrophobic. I can imagine her terror if she were to develop Lou Gehrig's disease, which progressively immobilizes patients while their cognitive faculties remain largely intact. For my mother, this would be a fate worse than death.

But still. I didn't feel comfortable with the idea of helping to shorten the life of a patient because of depression and resentment. In truth, I'm not sure I am comfortable with helping to intentionally hasten anyone's death for any reason. Does that make me a hypocrite?

I realized it was past time to sort out my thinking and turned to the de facto specialist in our area on this issue for counsel. Dr. Lonny Shavelson, an emergency medicine and primary care physician in Northern California, has been grappling with the subject for many years.

Given his interest in the topic, Dr. Shavelson felt a personal obligation to ensure that this new practice would be carried out responsibly after the law was passed. He founded Bay Area End of Life Options, a consulting group that educates physicians, advocates on patients' behalf and prescribes the lethal concoction for some patients who meet the criteria for participation.

He has devised a process for his patients that not only adheres to the letter of the law, but goes far beyond it. His patient intake procedures are time-consuming and include a thorough history and physical, extensive home visits, a review of medical records and discussions with the patients' doctors. He assesses the medical illness, the patient's mental and emotional state and family dynamics.

He does not offer the medications to most of the patients who request them, sometimes because he deems them more than six months away from death or because he is worried that they have been coerced or because he believes that severe depression is interfering with their judgment. Since starting his practice, he has been approached by 398 patients. He has accepted 79 of those into his program and overseen ingestion and death for 48.

Dr. Shavelson's careful observations have made him something of a bedside pharmacologist. In his experience, both the medications used and their dosages should be tailored to individual patients. While all patients enter a coma within minutes of ingesting the lethal cocktail, some deaths take longer, which can be distressing for the family and everyone else involved. One of his patients, a serious athlete, experienced a protracted death that Dr. Shavelson attributes to the patient's high cardiac function. After that experience, Dr. Shavelson began to obtain an athletic history on every patient, and to add stronger medications if indicated.

In another patient, a mesh stent had been deployed to keep his intestines from collapsing. This stent prevented absorption in key areas, slowing the effect of the drugs and prolonging his death. Dr. Shavelson now routinely asks about such stents, something that a doctor less experienced in this process might miss.

Dr. Shavelson strives to mitigate all symptoms and suffering before agreeing to assist any patient in dying. He recounted many cases where patients no longer requested the medications once their quality of life improved. He counts these cases among his greatest successes. This demonstrates that his commitment is to the patient, not the principle.

When I asked Dr. Shavelson how he might have proceeded with my patient, he said he would have tried everything to relieve his distress without using the lethal medication. But if in the end the patient still wanted to proceed, he would have obliged, presuming his depression was not so severe as to impair his judgment. "I don't have to agree with a patient's reasoning or conclusions," he said. "Those are hers to make, just as much as turning down chemotherapy or opting not to be intubated would be."

I recently called colleagues at other hospitals to learn how they were handling this law. Like me, most of them hadn't yet had much experience with it, but their involvement has mostly been positive. They described the few cases they had handled as "straightforward" — patients had carefully thought through the decision and had full family support. Most patients were enrolled in hospice care and supported throughout the ingestion process by trained personnel, almost always in their homes. My colleagues reported that they were free to opt out of the program if they were uncomfortable prescribing the medications. (Catholic health systems do not participate.)

Dr. Meredith Heller, director of inpatient palliative services at Kaiser Permanente San Francisco, said that while she understood my ambivalence, she herself felt significantly better about it than she had expected to. "Surprisingly, the vast majority of cases here have gone smoothly," she told me.

A little over a year after the law went into effect, I am heartened by the positive responses I am hearing from my colleagues around the state. I am relieved that most cases seem straightforward. I am grateful that there are dedicated physicians like Dr. Shavelson willing to do this work. And I am reassured by the knowledge that patients in California now have the legal right to exercise this power when they feel there is no other path.

But I am also concerned. As our population continues to grow older and sicker and more people learn that this law exists, we will need a highly trained work force to steward patients through this process.

My patient deserved an evaluation by a physician like Dr. Shavelson, not someone like me, with no training in this area and ambivalence to boot. We need formal protocols, official procedures, outcome measurements, even a certificate of expertise issued by an oversight board. None of these are in place in any participating state, according to Dr. Shavelson. Yet all medical procedures require training. Why should one this weighty be an exception?

What about payment? Providers can bill for an office visit and the cost of the medication. But because there are no specific codes established for this procedure, reimbursement doesn't come close to covering any effort to do this well. On top of that, many insurers won't cover it, including federal programs like Medicare and the Veterans Health Administration.

And will this new "right" be available to everyone? Most communities won't have a Dr. Shavelson, who offers steep discounts to low-income patients. I worry that public hospital patients like mine will not be able to afford this degree of care. These are inequities we must address.

There is another question I feel compelled to raise. Is medical aid in dying a reductive response to a highly complex problem? The over-mechanization of dying in America has created a public health crisis. People feel out of control around death. A life-ending concoction at the bedside can lend a sense of autonomy at a tremendously vulnerable time.

Yet medical aid in dying will help only a tiny fraction of the population. In 2016, just under four-tenths of 1 percent of everyone who died in Oregon used this option. Other approaches such as hospice and palliative care, proven to help a broad population of patients with life-limiting illness, are still underused, even stigmatized. The American Society of Clinical Oncology recommends that patients with advanced cancer receive concurrent palliative care beginning early in the course of disease. In my experience, far too few of these patients actually get it.

Unlike medical aid in dying, which will be used by a small proportion of the population, palliative interventions can improve the lives of many. My patient hadn't been seen by a palliative care physician before he made his request. Although recommended, it isn't required by law. And yet this input gave him another option.

Medical aid in dying is now the law in my home state, and I am glad for that. But our work is just beginning. We must continue to shape our policies and protocols to account for the nuanced social, legal and ethical questions that will continue to arise. We must identify the clinicians who are best qualified and most willing to do this work and then train them appropriately, not ad hoc. And we must remember that this is just one tool in the toolbox of caring for the dying — a tool of last resort.

JESSICA NUTIK ZITTER, a critical care and palliative medicine doctor at Highland Hospital, is the author of "Extreme Measures: Finding a Better Path to the End of Life."

Charlie Gard and Our Moral Confusion

OPINION | BY KENAN MALIK | JULY 19, 2017

LONDON — Two court cases in London this week expose the difficulties we have in thinking about what it means to die with dignity. In one, the parents of a seriously ill baby, Charlie Gard, are pleading for judges not to order their son's life support be turned off, but instead let him travel to the United States for experimental treatment. In the other, a terminally ill man, Noel Conway, suffering from motor neuron disease, wants the court to allow doctors to help him end his life at the moment of his choosing.

The tragic case of Charlie Gard has made international headlines, with both Pope Francis and President Trump offering their help. Charlie suffers from a rare genetic condition that prevents his cells from producing sufficient energy to maintain normal bodily functions. His major organs are failing and, according to Great Ormond Street Hospital, where he is being cared for, he has suffered "catastrophic and irreversible brain damage." He is on life support, which doctors believe should be switched off.

Charlie's parents, Connie Yates and Chris Gard, strongly disagree. They have pinned their hopes on an experimental treatment called nucleoside therapy. An American neurologist, Michio Hirano, of Columbia University Medical Center, has offered to treat Charlie, and his parents have raised about $1.7 million to fly him to America and pay for the treatment.

The disagreement between Charlie Gard's parents and the London hospital has ended up in the courts. Judges, both in Britain and at the European Court of Human Rights, have sided with the doctors. The High Court in London is considering new evidence about the efficacy of the treatment.

Some commentators have presented the case as one of religious norms about the sanctity of life pitted against a secular "throwaway culture" in which notions of "intrinsic worth are falling by the wayside." Yet the moral theologian Lisa Fullam has drawn on Catholic teachings to defend the decision to end Charlie's life, while the philosophers Julian Savulescu and Peter Singer, both noted secularist thinkers, have questioned the court rulings.

What makes the case particularly intractable is that there are valid arguments on both sides. Some moral questions have no single right answer. But if there is reason on both sides, there is also reason to question the judgments of the courts.

The courts have decided that it is not in Charlie Gard's "best interests" to receive further treatment and that he should be permitted "to die with dignity." Certainly, there are cases in which treatment may not be advisable — when, for instance, the possibility of success is vanishingly small, or when it may involve too great a degree of pain and suffering.

Charlie Gard's situation is different. According to Dr. Hirano, there is about a 10 percent chance of the treatment succeeding (to the extent that the child might gain some muscle strength and improved brain function). That may not be very high, but neither is it negligible. Charlie does not appear to be in severe pain, nor will he be as a consequence of the treatment.

Usually, a decision about a child's best interests involves two alternative futures. Is he better off with his mother or father after a divorce? Is it in his interests to stay with parents who may be having difficulties, or to be taken into care?

In Charlie Gard's case, though, the choice is between a possible future and a definite non-future. There is no future after death, and if life support is ended, Charlie will have no interest to debate.

It is more than six months since the courts first heard the case. A reasonable decision, one that acknowledges the complexities, might have been for the court to have accepted at the start that Charlie could receive treatment for a set period (say, three or six months). This would have permitted the treatment to be assessed, while all parties could have agreed that if the treatment did not succeed, the life support would be turned off. We would have known by now whether Charlie did possess an alternative future or whether his interest does lie in death.

In Charlie's case, the judges decided that it is in his interest to die even with a possibility of treatment. Mr. Conway, in contrast, wants to be allowed to die in dignity, but the law will not permit it. His motor neuron disease is incurable, and he is not expected to live beyond 12 months. His condition is painful, and will become more so. He wants doctors to be able to give him a lethal injection when he decides that it is time to end his life. Under British law, it would be a criminal offense for a doctor to do so.

Mr. Conway's case is the latest in a series of court challenges in Britain by terminally ill people who want to have the right to die on their terms and to have someone assist them in doing so. In 2015, Parliament rejected a bill modeled on the law in the state of Oregon that would have legalized assisted dying. Critics of the law worried that it would force doctors to abandon the Hippocratic oath, create a situation in which people might be pressured to take their lives and normalize suicide.

As in the Charlie Gard case, there are reasonable arguments on both sides of the debate. But it is difficult to divine the moral logic of insisting that Charlie must die with dignity, despite there being a possible treatment, and against the desperate pleas of his parents, while refusing to allow a terminally ill, morally competent individual that same right.

A rational, compassionate approach would surely accept that those able to exercise moral autonomy should be able to help determine what lies in their interests and how best to die with dignity, and that in cases in which individuals are unable to exercise autonomy, the state should acknowledge the difficulties in defining their best interest. It should also be particularly cautious about sanctioning death, especially when the experts are divided and parents are opposed.

It is a measure of our moral confusion that in Britain lawmakers and the courts have decided the very opposite.

KENAN MALIK is the author, most recently, of "The Quest for a Moral Compass: A Global History of Ethics" and a contributing opinion writer.

Let Dying People End Their Suffering

OPINION | BY DIANE REHM | JUNE 7, 2018

IT WAS AN EMOTIONAL MOMENT for my friend and for me. As we sat in the living room of her home in California, she told me that the breast cancer that had been responding to treatment for several years had spread throughout her body. "It's everywhere now," she said, adding without a trace of self-pity: "I have less than six months to live. I'm so grateful that I won't have to spend my last days or weeks in extreme agony."

She could tell me that because California's End of Life Options Act — supported by 76 percent of her fellow Californians, passed by the State Legislature and signed into law by Gov. Jerry Brown — had gone into effect on June 9, 2016. The law made it legal for doctors to prescribe drugs to end the lives of terminally ill patients, and my friend found solace in knowing she would have this choice. Her husband and children, who had seen her bear years of chemotherapy and other treatments and supported her as her pain intensified, wouldn't have to watch cancer torture her mercilessly as it took her life.

California's law was modeled after the one enacted in 1997 in Oregon, as were similar laws in Washington, Vermont, Colorado and, most recently, the District of Columbia and Hawaii; Montana also permits this end-of-life option as a result of a judicial decision rather than legislation.

But this source of comfort was ripped away from my friend and her family last month when a judge in Riverside County overturned the law on a technicality. His reasoning? The measure was passed during a special legislative session dedicated to health care issues, and complainants argued that it wasn't about health care.

Try telling that to my friend or the many others whose lives were upended by the decision of the judge, Daniel Ottolia. As opponents of the law cheer, she and her loved ones prepare for the anguish to come.

My children and I can empathize. In two weeks, we will mark the fourth anniversary of the death of John Rehm, my husband. He, too, had under six months to live and, he, too, was suffering to such a degree that he begged for medical aid in dying. But that option was not available in Maryland, where he was in an assisted living center. He ultimately chose to end his life by refusing to eat, drink and take medications. It took him 10 long and miserable days to die.

As in my friend's case, my husband was already going to die. He had Parkinson's disease, which left him unable to feed himself or do anything else without assistance. He did not choose what some insist upon labeling "suicide." Those who commit that act do not want to live. Most terminally ill patients like John would choose life if they could.

So today my friend and many other Californians are staring death in the face, without the degree of control over it that the End of Life Options Act briefly granted them. Some people will say they should place their faith in treatments to ease their pain. But despite the compassionate work of hospice and palliative care personnel, those treatments have their limits and cannot offer all patients the end-of-life experience they seek. Furthermore, as my friend told me, "I am the only one who can define when my suffering has become unbearable."

John's death reinforced my belief that medical aid in dying should be a choice available to all Americans. That's why I have been interviewing patients and doctors for a documentary on the subject, "When My Time Comes."

What's happening in California now is an unnecessary tragedy. Judge Ottolia's decision is being appealed, and a hearing will be held later this month. But it could take many months to play out in the courts — months during which dying patients will be denied the option to mitigate their pain and distress. The Legislature could reintroduce the measure and pass it anew — but that process will also take time.

I believe that this must and will be remedied. My confidence comes from the fact that individual Americans seeking autonomy are driving the national movement for medical aid in dying. Nearly three-quarters of Americans believe that terminally ill patients should have that option.

Let me be clear: I understand that many people believe that only God should determine the time of their death, and I support them 100 percent. Others want every additional minute of life that medical science can give them, and I support those people 100 percent. But the end of life is an extremely personal experience. If, when my time comes, I see only unbearable suffering ahead of me, then I want my preference to have access to medical aid in dying to be supported 100 percent, as well.

As Archbishop Desmond Tutu has written, "Regardless of what you might choose for yourself, why should you deny others the right to make this choice?"

The California law was allowing patients that choice. Its nullification is causing them cruel and unnecessary torment.

DIANE REHM, who hosted "The Diane Rehm Show" on NPR for 37 years, is a producer of the forthcoming documentary "When My Time Comes" and host of the podcast "On My Mind." Ms. Rehm's husband died four years ago.

The Death of the Doctor's Dog

BY BARRON H. LERNER, M.D. | FEB. 6, 2018

OUR DOG'S BRAIN TUMOR had worsened to the point that she was restless at all times and often walked in circles. She had mostly stopped eating and was partially blind. Like so many pet owners, our family finally decided to intervene rather than having "nature take its course."

Akeela, our beloved boxer, had had her share of medical problems over the years, including a ruptured liver tumor and surgery for a parathyroid adenoma. But after the age of 12, she developed both a severe hormonal abnormality known as Cushing's disease and a brain tumor that caused seizures.

Our girl dutifully kept going, willingly taking a very large amount of medications. But by this past September, her symptoms, which were probably caused by the spread of the tumor, had worsened.

The veterinarian took one look at Akeela and said, "This is not a happy dog." We had to concur. The very traits that had once made her so distinctive — her joy, her displays of affection, her constant monitoring of the house — had waned.

My wife and two adult children and I held a family meeting. After some discussion, we agreed it was time to put her down and selected a date and a venue — our home. In the next couple of days, my children's friends, our longtime nanny and many others who loved Akeela visited and said their goodbyes. There were a lot of tears, which we tried to hide from her.

The veterinarian who came to the house was very professional; she specializes in at-home euthanasia. Having heard the story and met Akeela, she concurred with our assessment.

The process of euthanasia involves two injections — one to sedate the dog and a second to stop the heart. Apparently, some dogs become agitated by the first injection, but Akeela quickly became very sleepy.

"She's tired," the veterinarian said.

As a physician, I was skeptical that Akeela's response to the sedative truly indicated whether it was time for her to go. But on an emotional level, what the vet had said made sense. Because of her Cushing's, Akeela had been panting on and off for months. And the worsening restlessness and circling had to have been taxing for her.

I took Akeela's death hard. I truly believe that relieving her suffering was the humane thing to do.

But what did Akeela's end say about my own practice of medicine?

In contrast to veterinary practice, the medical profession has long forbidden the notion of speeding death. The Hippocratic oath, which dates to Greece in the fifth century B.C., states that a physician must not "administer a poison to anybody when asked to do so nor ... suggest such a course."

Instances in which physicians have participated in euthanasia have generally been wholly unethical. These include a program started by Nazi physicians in the 1930s to kill mentally ill and chronically infirm persons and over 100 controversial deaths facilitated in the 1990s by Dr. Jack Kevorkian, a pathologist who believed that terminal patients had a right to determine when they died.

There is one current exception to the prohibition on physicians expediting death: physician aid-in-dying. In six states and Washington, D.C., physicians may legally prescribe medications that terminally ill patients may take when they so wish. Numerous protections are written into these laws, such as making sure that the person is really dying and has full capacity to make decisions.

I could think of stories similar to that of Akeela among my own patients. There was the blind woman who was bedbound, in pain and partially paralyzed from a stroke; another woman was skeletal from metastatic cancer and required constant sedation and analgesia. There have been many more. Some of these patients had explicitly expressed a wish to die, hoping that we doctors might, humanely, "end it all."

My experiences with Akeela led me to reflect on these cases. If suffering was so obvious and not reversible, and there was a way to provide immediate relief, was my reflexive refusal to assist in the dying process always the right thing to do? And if the patient, fully understanding all of his or her options, was asking for death, didn't this make him or her more worthy than a dog, whose suffering could only be assumed? I had little doubt that family members, seeing a loved one suddenly at peace, might have said what our vet said to us: "She was tired."

But in my own practice, I can never countenance euthanasia. Hippocrates' sentiments from over 2,000 years ago resonate for me. Doctors are in the business of healing bodies, not harming them — even if that "harm" potentially provides relief from the same type of suffering we find unacceptable in our pets.

Having said this, I am not opposed to telling my patients about physician aid-in-dying. Indeed, were they so inclined and prepared to move to a state where it is legal, I might help them make the transition. And if aid-in-dying became legal in my own state, New York, I would consider making a referral to a physician who might prescribe the necessary drugs.

Of course, for most patients, moving to another state near life's end is neither desirable nor practical. And in many cases, the process could never be implemented in time. Fortunately, though, there are now better medications to treat the symptoms of dying and a specialty, known as palliative care, that can provide expert guidance in doing so.

BARRON H. LERNER, an internist and historian at New York University Langone Medical Center, is the author of "The Good Doctor: A Father, A Son and the Evolution of Medical Ethics."

A Debate Over 'Rational Suicide'

BY PAULA SPAN | AUG. 31, 2018

ON A MARCH MORNING in 1989, Robert Shoots was found dead in his garage in Weir, Kan. He had run a tube from the tailpipe of his beloved old Chrysler to the front seat, where he sat with a bottle of Wild Turkey. He was 80.

His daughter wishes he had mentioned this plan when they spoke by phone the night before, because she didn't get to say a satisfying goodbye. But she would not have tried to dissuade him from suicide.

Years earlier, he had told her of his intentions.

"It wasn't a big surprise," she said of his death. "I knew what he was going to do and how he was going to do it." (Wary of harassment in her conservative upstate New York town, she has asked me to withhold her name.)

Mr. Shoots, a retired house painter, was happily remarried and enjoyed good health. He still went fishing and played golf, showing no signs of the depression or other mental illness that afflicts most people who take their own lives.

Nevertheless, he had explained why he someday planned to take his life. "All the people he knew were dying in hospitals, full of tubes, lying there for weeks, and he was just horrified by it," his daughter said. He was determined to avoid that kind of death.

Is suicide by older adults ever a rational choice? It's a topic many older people discuss among themselves, quietly or loudly — and one that physicians increasingly encounter, too. Yet most have scant training or experience in how to respond, said Dr. Meera Balasubramaniam, a geriatric psychiatrist at the New York University School of Medicine.

"I found myself coming across individuals who were very old, doing well, and shared that they wanted to end their lives at some point," said Dr. Balasubramaniam. "So many of our patients are confronting this in their heads."

She has not taken a position on whether suicide can be rational — her views are "evolving," she said. But hoping to generate more medical discussion, she and a co-editor explored the issue in a 2017 anthology, "Rational Suicide in the Elderly," and she revisited it recently in an article in the Journal of the American Geriatrics Society.

The Hastings Center, the ethics institute in Garrison, N.Y., also devoted much of its latest Hastings Center Report to a debate over "voluntary death" to forestall dementia.

Every part of this idea, including the very phrase "rational suicide," remains intensely controversial. (Let's leave aside the related but separate issue of physician aid in dying, currently legal in seven states and the District of Columbia, which applies only to mentally competent people likely to die of a terminal illness within six months.)

Suicide has already become a pressing public health concern for older adults, more than 8,200 of whom took their lives in 2016, according to the Centers for Disease Control and Prevention.

"Older people in general, and older men specifically, have the highest rates," said Dr. Yeates Conwell, a geriatric psychiatrist at the University of Rochester School of Medicine and a longtime suicide researcher.

That's true even though research consistently shows older adults feeling happier than younger ones, with improved mental health.

A complex web of conditions contributes to late-life suicide, including physical illness and functional decline, personality traits and coping styles, and social disconnection.

But the vast majority of older people who kill themselves also have a diagnosable mental illness, primarily depression, Dr. Conwell pointed out.

Suicide often also involves impulsivity, rather than careful consideration. That doesn't fit anybody's definition of a rational act.

"The suicidal state is not fixed," Dr. Conwell said. "It's a teeter-totter. There's a will to live and a will to die, and it goes back and forth."

When health care providers aggressively treat seniors' depression and work to improve their health, function and relationships, he said, "it can change the equation."

Failing to take action to prevent suicide, some ethicists and clinicians argue, reflects an ageist assumption — one older people themselves aren't immune to — that the lives of old or disabled people lack value.

A tolerant approach also overlooks the fact that people often change their minds, declaring certain conditions unendurable in the abstract but choosing to live when the worst actually happens.

Slippery-slope arguments factor into the debate, too. "We worry that we could shift from a right to die to a duty to die if we make suicide seem desirable or justifiable," Dr. Balasubramaniam said.

But the size of the baby boomer cohort, with the drive for autonomy that has characterized its members, means that doctors expect more of their older patients to contemplate controlling the time and manner of their deaths.

Not all of them are depressed or otherwise impaired in judgment.

"Perhaps you feel your life is on a downhill course," said Dena Davis, a bioethicist at Lehigh University who has written about what she calls "pre-emptive suicide."

"You've completed the things you wanted to do. You see life's satisfactions getting smaller and the burdens getting larger — that's true for a lot of us as our bodies start breaking down."

At that point, "it might be rational to end your life," Dr. Davis continued. "Unfortunately, in the world we currently live in, if you don't take control of life's end, it's likely to go in ways that are inimical to your wishes."

Dr. Davis cared for her mother as she slowly succumbed to Alzheimer's disease. She intends to avoid a similar death, a decision she has discussed with her son, her friends and her doctor.

"We ought to start having conversations that challenge the taboo" of suicide, she said.

However heated the arguments become, as religious groups and disability activists and right-to-die proponents weigh in, there's agreement on that point, at least. Reflexively negative reactions to an older person's mere mention of suicide — Don't say that! — shut down dialogue.

"Discussing it doesn't mean you're advocating it," Dr. Balasubramaniam said.

Her training has taught her that suicide is preventable. But she also sees her role — one family and friends can play, too — as listening carefully to patients who discuss an eventual suicide, even as she looks for treatable illnesses that might be impacting their thinking.

"Sitting with someone who understands, who communicates caring, who is listening, is itself a reason for living," Dr. Conwell said.

But not for everyone.

Mr. Shoot's daughter watched her mother die of Alzheimer's, too, and shares her father's conviction that some fates are worse than death.

She has told her four children that she intends to die before her life deteriorates to levels she finds intolerable; they accept her decision, she said.

Accordingly, she avoids tests like mammograms and colonoscopies because she won't treat the diseases they reveal. To celebrate her 70th birthday, she had the initials D.N.R. — for Do Not Resuscitate — tattooed on her chest, within a decorative circle.

For now, she enjoys her semirural life, but she monitors herself closely for signs of cognitive and functional decline. "When I start to slip too much," she said, "it's time."

CHAPTER 2

Ethical, Legal and Political Issues

As experts debate the ethics behind assisted suicide, individual cases and amendments have made their way through the American legal system, resulting in a series of court cases and state laws that both open up and restrict the availability of assisted suicide. In this chapter, the following articles speak to the increasing legal acceptance of assisted suicide and how these cases have evolved over time.

In Oregon, Choosing Death Over Suffering

BY JOHN SCHWARTZ AND JAMES ESTRIN | JUNE 1, 2004

ARTHUR W. WILSON sits in his study, breathing oxygen through a nose clip and pausing frequently for the coughs that rack his body.

"I'm not suicidal," he said. "I'm sane."

Mr. Wilson, 86, has been living with the profound pain of chronic obstructive pulmonary disease for years. Now he wants to end his life — not today, not tomorrow, but when he chooses — under the provisions of Oregon's Death With Dignity law.

"When the time comes," he said, "I'm going to swallow that bottle of Lethe and say goodbye."

He is no stranger to death, having fought in World War II and in Korea. And he craves being in control. His house is snaked through with a clear plastic tubing system that he devised to carry his oxygen from room to room without having to drag a tank around behind him.

He does not seem, in other words, to be the depressed, languishing patient many might expect to see applying for the Oregon program.

The state's law allows adults with terminal diseases who are likely to die within six months to obtain lethal doses of drugs from their doctors. In the six years since it went into effect, surprises have been common, including the small number of people who have sought lethal drugs under the law and the even smaller number of people who have actually used them. In surveys and conversations with counselors, many patients say that what they want most is a choice about how their lives will end, a finger on the remote control, as it were.

Last week, the United States Court of Appeals for the Ninth Circuit upheld Oregon's law, ruling that Attorney General John Ashcroft had overstepped his authority in trying to punish doctors who prescribed suicide drugs under the law.

And while there is still strong opposition around the country to laws like Oregon's, support within the state has grown over the years. Oregon voters passed the law in two separate referendums. Even some former opponents say the widespread abuses predicted by some have not emerged. And studies are helping researchers and policymakers understand how it really works in practice.

Perhaps the most surprising thing to emerge from Oregon is how rarely the law has actually been used.

"We estimate that one out of a hundred individuals who begin the process of asking about assisted suicide will carry it out," said Ann Jackson, executive director of the Oregon Hospice Association.

Since 1997, 171 patients with terminal illnesses have legally taken their own lives using lethal medication, compared with 53,544 Oregonians with the same diseases who died from other causes during that time, according to figures released by the Oregon Department of Health Services in March.

More than 100 people begin the process of requesting the drugs in a typical year. Doctors wrote 67 prescriptions for the drugs in 2003, up from 24 in 1998. Forty-two patients died under the law in 2003 compared with 16 in 1998.

Many patients say they want to have the option to end their lives if the pain becomes unbearable or if they are sliding into incompetence while still thinking clearly.

"I'd say it's less than 50-50 that I'd ever do this thing," said Don James, a retired school administrator with advanced prostate cancer who has not yet received his pills.

A DESIRE TO BE IN CONTROL

A second surprise has been the kind of people who use the law. They are not so much depressed as determined, said Linda Ganzini, a professor of psychiatry at Oregon Health Sciences University. She led a recent survey of 35 doctors who had received requests for suicide drugs. The doctors described the patients as "feisty" and "unwavering."

A third lesson is that for most of those who seek assisted suicide, the greatest concern appears not to be fear of pain but fear of losing autonomy, which is cited by 87 percent of the people who have taken their lives with the drugs. Only 22 percent of the patients listed fear of inadequate pain control as an end-of-life concern, perhaps a sign that pain management has improved over the years.

And though opponents of the law argued that patients would feel pressured by families and even insurers to end their lives early out of financial concerns, so far concerns of being a burden to family have been cited by 36 percent of patients, and financial concerns by just 2 percent. The surveys show that the standard version of health care for terminally ill patients might not be what these patients are looking for, Dr. Ganzini said. The standard version of care says, in effect, "we're going to take care of you," she said. But "for them, the real problem is other people taking care of you."

Ms. Jackson said the surveys were changing the hospice association's practices.

In 1994, the group opposed the Death With Dignity law. Now the hospices work directly with programs like Compassion in Dying, a group that is involved in 75 percent of Oregon's assisted suicides. Thanks to the surveys of patients seeking assisted suicide, Ms. Jackson said, her organization learned that half the people who rejected hospice care did so because "they thought that hospice was condescending or arrogant."

Now the hospices fit their treatments to patients who seek assisted suicide and emphasize that their wishes will be respected, she said.

Opponents of the Oregon law like Dr. Kenneth Stevens, chairman of the department of radiation oncology at the Oregon Health and Science University in Portland, say it violates the fundamental tenet of medicine. Dr. Stevens argues that doctors should not assist in suicides because to do so is incompatible with the doctor's role as healer.

"I went into medicine to help people," he said. "I didn't go into medicine to give people a prescription for them to die."

Dr. Stevens heads an organization, Physicians for Compassionate Care, that opposes assisted suicide and the Oregon law. Members of his group, he said, tend to be "people of faith," who believe that assisted suicide violates their religious principles. But they base their opposition to the law on moral and ethical grounds, arguing that it leads down a slippery slope toward euthanasia and patient abuses.

He recalled the struggle of his wife, who died of cancer in 1982. In the weeks before she died, he said, her doctor offered her an "extra-large prescription" for painkillers.

"As I helped her into the car, she said, 'He wants me to kill myself,' " Dr. Stevens recalled. "It just devastated her that her doctor, her trusted doctor, subtly suggested that."

Others who initially opposed the law, like the hospice group, say they have learned to live with it. Michael Bailey, for example, took out a loan in 1994 to fight the Death With Dignity act. His daughter has

Down syndrome, and he said that at the time he could see a straight line between voluntary assisted suicide and forced euthanasia for the handicapped.

Now Mr. Bailey says he has not seen any abuses. "I don't see that there's ever been a scandal," he said, "and the numbers are not huge." Still, he does not support the law. "If it was up to me, I'd say no, but I don't think there's any great human rights crisis here," he said.

Support for the law crosses ideological lines, said Nicholas van Aelstyn, a lawyer in San Francisco who works with Compassion in Dying. Some commentators have characterized the movement as a liberal cause, but "to most of the people exercising it, it's a libertarian issue," he said. "Many of our clients are die-hard Republicans who don't want government interfering in their lives."

That certainly describes Mr. Wilson, who calls himself a "staunch conservative" and says Mr. Ashcroft is "dead wrong" about the Oregon law.

The support for the law in Oregon, Mr. James said, reflects the pioneer spirit that flows from the wagon trains that brought the early settlers. "They were pretty well-educated, family-oriented people willing to hack a new life out of this wilderness," he said. "Pretty independent folks."

Those who drafted the Death With Dignity Act say they did not try to come up with a political document that would warm the heart of Jack Kevorkian, or that would permit euthanasia, which is repugnant to a significant portion of the population. Instead, they say, they carefully drew up a law that they believed would gain the support of everyone except the most determined opponents, and that was loaded with safeguards against abuse.

Doctors have long made lethal doses of drugs available to patients inclined to end their struggle against disease, said Eli Stutsman, president of the board of the Death With Dignity National Center.

"We took something that was already happening, and we wrote a law around it," he said.

Opponents had argued that Oregon would become a magnet for people seeking suicide, so the law's provisions were restricted to the state's residents.

The law also sets a high barrier to getting the life-ending medications, giving patients the chance to change their mind up to the last moment. A patient must make two oral requests for the drugs and one written request after a 15-day waiting period. Two doctors must determine that the patient has less than six months to live, a doctor must decide that the patient is capable of making independent decisions about health care and the doctor has to describe to the patient alternatives like hospice care.

The law also requires that the drugs be self-administered by the patient, rather than given by a doctor or family member, to avoid involuntary euthanasia. The death certificate, under the law, must state the cause of death as the underlying disease, not suicide.

That provision pleases Mr. James.

"I don't like the word 'suicide,' " he said, because "if I'm really on a path, the natural path" toward death, and "just hastening it a little bit, I don't call that suicide."

Mr. Wilson's family supports him in his wishes, although his wife, Viola, says she is against the general idea.

"This is his thing, not mine," she said. "It's not the way I'd go."

Her views flow from her religious beliefs, she said.

"I'm inclined to think that I have a purpose in life until I go," she said. "God has a plan for me, and I'm here until he says it's time to go."

She said she liked her husband's idea of having family members gather in a kind of living wake, however.

"That would be fine," she said. "You should celebrate the life instead of worry about the death."

A LAST GOODBYE

Although the idea of an end-of-life celebration strikes some people as unseemly or exhibitionist for a most private act, many patients say it is natural to want to bring family together for a last goodbye. Most patients call for such a gathering, although relatively few take the poison in the presence of their families.

Barbara Coombs Lee, the president of Compassion in Dying Federation, said she saw the suicides not as "an impulse to self destruction," but as "an impulse to self preservation — preservation of the self I cherish."

That point of view clearly grates on Dr. Stevens. Although he said he did not want to "put people down or label people," he added, "the 'P' word is not 'pain.' The 'P' word is 'pride.' " He explained, "Rather than being death with dignity, it's death with vanity."

But Dr. Marcia Angell, a former executive editor of The New England Journal of Medicine and a supporter of doctor-assisted suicide, said: "He can call it vanity. Somebody else might call it admirable independence."

If anything, Dr. Angell said, the Oregon law may be too restrictive and may not reach everyone who could benefit from it.

"I am concerned that so few people are requesting it," she said. "It seems to me that more would do it. The purpose of a law is to be used, not to sit there on the books."

Mr. Stutsman, one of the law's authors, said it helped people who never end up holding a cup of barbiturate solution in their hands.

"They get the comfort of knowing that the Oregon Death With Dignity Act is there if they need it," he said. Although no state has passed its own version of the act, "Oregon is leading the national debate," he said.

Compassion in Dying claims that the Oregon law prevents violent suicides and the pain such deaths cause families. The patients say, however, that to some extent, the 10-year furor over the law is academic; it is not so hard to die, and people do it around the world without the benefit of laws like that passed by the Oregon Legislature.

Mr. James, for example, said, "If it gets too bad, I might just stop eating," and refers jokingly to his "Ashcroft kit," a sturdy plastic bag and a roll of duct tape that he could use to asphyxiate himself. But, he added, that would be illegal, and "I just think that's bad karma to do it that way."

Other patients say they know a good death from a bad death, and know which kind they prefer. Lovelle Svart, a retired newspaper librarian, said she recently witnessed a horrifying auto accident on the highway.

"Not that way," she recalled saying to herself. "Not the way I want to go."

Arrests Draw New Attention to Assisted Suicide

BY ROBBIE BROWN | MARCH 10, 2009

ATLANTA — An undercover state investigator told a right-to-die network that he wanted to kill himself. In response, he later testified, officials of the network planned to have him asphyxiate himself with a helium-filled face mask while holding down his arms.

After an investigation, four officials of the group, known as the Final Exit Network, were arrested last month on charges of racketeering and assisted suicide.

The arrests raised questions about whether the group, which has helped some 200 people commit suicide since 2004, merely watched people take the leap into death, or pushed them over the edge.

Officials with the Georgia Bureau of Investigation say the network, which says it has 3,000 dues-paying members in the United States, actively takes part in suicides, an act that is illegal in every state except Oregon and Washington. "The law is clear, and they violated it," said John Bankhead, a spokesman for the Georgia bureau.

The arrests followed an inquiry in which an investigator posed as a cancer patient and persuaded network members to help him prepare to commit suicide.

According to the agent's affidavit, network members instructed him to buy a helium tank and a plastic "exit mask."

Thomas E. Goodwin, who was the network president at the time, and Claire Blehr, a member, planned to hold down the agent's hands while helium flowed into the mask, the affidavit says.

The agent would lose consciousness within seconds and die within minutes, and the guides would remove evidence from the scene.

"They went through a dry run just to let the agent know what would happen," Mr. Bankhead said. "Mr. Goodwin got on top of the agent and held down both of his hands," which investigators say would have prevented him from removing the mask if he had changed his mind during a real suicide.

Georgia authorities arrested Mr. Goodwin and Ms. Blehr, and Maryland officials arrested the group's medical director, Dr. Lawrence D. Egbert, and a regional coordinator, Nicholas Alec Sheridan, for authorizing member suicides.

The network, based in Marietta, Ga., says it provides only lawful instruction and emotional support, and only to patients with incurable diseases or tremendous suffering.

"Assisted suicide is Jack Kevorkian putting a needle in someone with a deadly substance," said Jerry Dincin, who became the network president after the arrests. "We provide information that we think is protected under the First Amendment."

A 1994 Georgia law defines assisted suicide as "direct and physical involvement, intervention or participation" in a deliberate suicide and carries a five-year prison sentence.

The arrests have thrust the little-known organization into the national spotlight. Since its founding in 2004, the network has neither shunned public attention nor received much of it.

A registered nonprofit organization, the group runs a Web site, promotes a suicide manual by Derek Humphry, the chairman of the network's advisory board, and belongs to the World Federation of Right to Die Societies.

Network literature says members receive services including "counseling, support and even guidance" on suicide, in exchange for an annual $50 fee.

The group also sends trained "exit guides" to provide comfort and instruction during a suicide but is adamant that members buy their own materials and conduct the suicide themselves.

While political and educational groups like the Death With Dignity National Center and Compassion and Choices work with lawmakers to advance physician-assisted suicide, the Final Exit Network ministers directly to the suicidal.

Other groups are concerned that the network will portray the movement negatively.

"People don't want to do this underground or covertly, with hushed tones, with great risks to themselves and their loved ones," said Barbara Coombs Lee, the president of Compassion and Choices, which supports end-of-life decisions. "They want to have their physician involved. They want hospice care involved. They want their family there without shame or risk."

If brought to trial, legal experts say, the case against the network could clarify the distinctions between the lawful act of witnessing a suicide and the illegal act of assisting one.

The Supreme Court ruled in 2006 that states can set their own laws on suicide assistance. But experts say the term "assistance" can be difficult to define.

"You have some in our society saying this action is a crime," said William H. Colby, a lawyer and fellow of the Center for Practical Bioethics. "You have others saying this is such an important right that it rises to the level of our Constitution."

Mr. Humphry said the network's protocols were deliberately written to avoid illegality. "The person does everything themselves," he said. "They don the hood. They tie it around their neck. They reach forward. They turn on the gas."

Guides often hold a dying person's hands, he said, but for support, not restraint.

Supporters are concerned that the network arrests will set back the right-to-die movement. Mr. Kevorkian, the Michigan pathologist who served eight years in prison for second-degree murder for assisting a suicide, issued a statement on Tuesday through his lawyer supporting the right to physician-assisted suicide but condemning its practice by "ordinary citizens" in the network.

Opponents of assisted suicide were harsher.

"These are people who instead of pulling you back from the ledge, they shove you off," said Stephen Drake, a research analyst for Not

Dead Yet, an advocacy group for the disabled that opposes assisted suicide. "Legally, we may not know what this means. But in a personal sense, it can mean the difference between life and death."

The investigation began after relatives of a Georgia man, John Celmer, who committed suicide in June, told the police they believed that the network had taken part in Mr. Celmer's death.

Mr. Celmer's mother said her son had long suffered from mouth and throat cancer, but Georgia investigators said he had overcome the disease by the time he killed himself and was instead embarrassed about a facial disfigurement.

His wife, Susan, issued a statement of gratitude to the law enforcement officials who "pursued this matter vigorously."

Mr. Dincin, the network president, said Mr. Celmer deserved the right to end his suffering.

"There are millions of people who think what we do is just awful," Mr. Dincin said. "They think we shouldn't touch a person's natural course from living to dying, but I think people have a right to decide for themselves."

A Polarizing Figure in End-of-Life Debates

BY JOHN SCHWARTZ | JUNE 4, 2011

IN REPORTS OF Dr. Jack Kevorkian's death on Friday at the age of 83, the general rule of obituaries held: Do not speak ill of the dead.

Dr. Kevorkian was generally described as a difficult man who helped advance the cause of assisted suicide for those with terminal illness.

Within the movement known generally as death with dignity, however, the evaluation of his contribution might seem surprisingly qualified, and the praise decidedly muted.

"He raised the profile of the issue, but he put the wrong face on it," said Eli D. Stutsman, a lawyer in Portland, Ore., who helped draft his state's trailblazing Death With Dignity Act, which allows terminal patients to end their own lives with the help of a doctor.

The 1997 Oregon law was built with compromise and careful consideration of policy, Mr. Stutsman said. It includes requirements that the patient be at the end stage of terminal disease and not have psychiatric disorders like depression, and that the patient take the drugs used in the procedure without help, to ensure that the act is voluntary from start to finish.

It is a very different system from that of Dr. Kevorkian, who seemed to make up his methods as he went along. He did not appear to screen patients to determine whether they were actually close to death, and he seemed to make no efforts to get counseling for those who might have wanted to live longer.

He devised "suicide machines" that could deliver drugs or carbon monoxide gas and could be set off by the patients. He carted the equipment to patients in his battered Volkswagen van and left many of the resulting 130 or more bodies at emergency rooms or even in hotel rooms.

Death, certainly — but death with dignity, no.

"Under the Oregon Death with Dignity Act, we would have put him in jail," Mr. Stutsman said. "We ended up using him as an example of how not to do it."

Since the act was passed, 525 people have ended their lives under its auspices, according to the state's 2010 annual report. In 2010, 96 prescriptions were written for the barbiturates used, and 65 people ended their lives.

Mr. Stutsman went on to be a founding board member of the Death With Dignity National Center, which promotes similar legislative efforts around the country. They face serious opposition by groups that reject physician-assisted suicide for reasons that include religious belief and concern that such laws would open the door to forced euthanasia.

Mr. Stutsman said successful campaigns in Oregon and Washington State showed the value of a strategy of compromise and coalition building.

"He was advocating from the margins of the political debate," Mr. Stutsman said of Dr. Kevorkian. "I was working from the middle of the political continuum — it's very hard to change public policy from the margins of the debate."

The movement won a major victory in 2006 when the United States Supreme Court ruled that the federal government could not prosecute Oregon doctors who participated in the assisted-suicide law.

Peg Sandeen, the executive director of the Death With Dignity National Center, said the ruling helped convince states that their own efforts would be respected — and was, she said, a major factor in the 2008 passage of the Washington State bill.

The Montana Supreme Court held in 2009 that no state law restricts the right of its citizens to end their lives with the help of physicians, though the court did not go so far as to say that physician-assisted suicide is a right under the State Constitution.

Efforts so far in California, Hawaii, Maine and Vermont have not been successful, though a new bill is before the Vermont Legislature.

Barbara Coombs Lee, the president of Compassion and Choices, a group that promotes what it refers to as "end-of-life choice" in legislatures and the courts and was a co-plaintiff in the Montana case, said Dr. Kevorkian "was quite scornful of any effort to change the law."

She called his death "the end of an era."

Noting that he was a polarizing figure — "people either thought he was a saint and martyred or the devil incarnate" — she explained, "To us, he was neither, but certainly pivotal to our movement."

Even at the extremes, she said, he "raised everyone's consciousness about the problem of end-of-life suffering" and spurred others to look for ways for those with terminal illness to end their lives on their own terms.

An "ignominious" death at the hands of Dr. Kevorkian "was a dramatic display of just how desperate people were who are seeking a peaceful end of their terminal disease," she said.

The policy-oriented groups worked to distinguish themselves from the Kevorkian spectacle. One Washington briefing in 1999 was titled "Jack Kevorkian and Physician-Assisted Dying: Not One and the Same."

Still, disagreement has its uses, said Scott Blaine Swenson, who was the executive director of the Death With Dignity National Center from 2001 to 2005. "He was the perfect foil" for the centrist movement that was promoting policy change, Mr. Swenson said. "You need somebody to play against," he said.

Dr. Kevorkian — erratic, loud and playing by his own rules — helped the movement establish rules that voters could live with, Mr. Swenson said.

"The truth, I think, is that had a Kevorkian not existed, that folks in Oregon and other proponents of assisted dying would have needed to invent him," he said.

'Aid in Dying' Movement Takes Hold in Some States

BY ERIK ECKHOLM | FEB. 7, 2014

DENVER — Helping the terminally ill end their lives, condemned for decades as immoral, is gaining traction. Banned everywhere but Oregon until 2008, it is now legal in five states. Its advocates, who have learned to shun the term "assisted suicide," believe that as baby boomers watch frail parents suffer, support for what they call the "aid in dying" movement will grow further.

In January, a district court in New Mexico authorized doctors to provide lethal prescriptions and declared a constitutional right for "a competent, terminally ill patient to choose aid in dying." Last May, the Vermont Legislature passed a law permitting it, joining Montana, Oregon and Washington. This spring, advocates are

MATTHEW STAVER FOR THE NEW YORK TIMES

Robert Mitton, 58, whose heart is failing, has become a proponent of the idea that people should be able to get help dying.

strongly promoting "death with dignity" bills in Connecticut and other states.

Public support for assisted dying has grown in the past half-century but depends in part on terminology. In a Gallup Poll conducted in May, for example, 70 percent of respondents agreed that when patients and their families wanted it, doctors should be allowed to "end the patient's life by some painless means." In 1948, that share was 37 percent, and it rose steadily for four decades but has remained roughly stable since the mid-1990s.

Yet in the same 2013 poll, only 51 percent supported allowing doctors to help a dying patient "commit suicide."

About 3,000 patients a year, from every state, contact the advocacy group Compassion & Choices for advice on legal ways to reduce end-of-life suffering and perhaps hasten their deaths.

Giving a fading patient the opportunity for a peaceful and dignified death is not suicide, the group says, which it defines as an act by people with severe depression or other mental problems.

But overt assistance to bring on death, by whatever name, remains illegal in most of the country. And so for Robert Mitton of Denver, 58 and with a failing heart, the news from New Mexico last month was bittersweet.

"I am facing my imminent death," he said, asking why people in Montana and New Mexico "are able to die with dignity and I am not."

"This should be a basic human right."

Husky and garrulous, with a graying ponytail, Mr. Mitton does not look like a dying man. But his doctors say that he must undergo extensive open-heart surgery in the coming months or face a nearly certain and painful end.

A previous operation to replace his aortic valve was so brutal, he says, that now, with his prior implant failing, he will not endure the surgery again. He wants a doctor's help to end his life before he becomes too helpless to act.

Mr. Mitton's frustrated quest draws attention to the limited choices facing patients in the large majority of states that bar the practice.

Opponents say that actively ending a life, no matter how frail a person is, is a moral violation and that patients might be pushed to die early for the convenience of others.

"The church teaches that life is sacred from conception through to natural death," Archbishop Michael J. Sheehan of Santa Fe, N.M., told legislators at a recent breakfast as he criticized the court decision there.

"This assisted-suicide thing concerns me," Archbishop Sheehan added, according to The New Mexican. "I foresee dangerous consequences."

Mr. Mitton's predicament illustrates a seldom-discussed side of the debate: the anguish experienced, and the sometimes desperate measures taken, by some patients in states where doctors who knowingly prescribe lethal drugs, or relatives who help a patient obtain them, can be subject to felony charges of "assisted suicide."

Oregon's Death With Dignity Act, which took effect in 1997, authorized prescriptions for lethal doses when two doctors agree that a patient will die within six months and is freely choosing this path.

More than a decade passed before another state followed suit. In 2008, voters in Washington approved a similar law. In 2012, after a political battle, voters in Massachusetts narrowly defeated such a measure. But last May, the Vermont Legislature approved one.

In response to lawsuits, state courts in Montana in 2009 and now New Mexico have said that aid in dying is legal, distinguishing it from the crime of assisted suicide.

By law and medical standards, only genuine residents who have relationships with local doctors can qualify for the prescriptions in any of these states, so patients like Mr. Mitton cannot move in at the last minute.

There is a quiet, constant demand all over the country for a right to die on one's own terms, said Barbara Coombs Lee, president of Compassion & Choices, and that demand is likely to grow, she said, as the baby boomers age.

Her group counsels people who call for advice, Ms. Lee said, describing options but not encouraging them to end their lives or providing direct help.

Callers who seem to be mentally disturbed and suicidal, she said, are referred to a suicide hotline. If they are facing imminent suffering and death and seek some control, the group urges them first to arrange for palliative or hospice care as they consider their next steps.

"People should get the best care, but also have a choice to accelerate the time of death if the very best care cannot make their remaining days acceptable," she said.

One method for some is to simply halt vital treatments, such as dialysis or insulin. Another is to turn off a pacemaker or, like Mr. Mitton, refuse an unwanted new treatment. An increasingly popular choice, she said — "for patients who are truly, emotionally and spiritually ready to die" — is to stop eating and drinking.

Others try to accumulate medications that would bring a peaceful death.

But it makes a tremendous difference, Ms. Lee said, to live where the law permits assisted dying. Too often people seek alternatives in shame and secrecy, sometimes making frantic international trips for lethal drugs or using more violent means to kill themselves.

Research in Oregon indicates that for many patients, just knowing the option is there has proved a great comfort, she noted. Of the 122 patients who obtained lethal drugs in 2013, only 71 used them, the rest dying naturally with the pills in a drawer.

Mr. Mitton is an unusual case because, unlike the more typical candidates with advanced cancer or A.L.S., he is refusing a potentially lifesaving procedure that would be covered by public insurance. He suffered heart damage from rheumatic fever in his teens. In 1999, in an open-heart operation followed by an unusually rough recovery, doctors replaced his failing aortic valve with one made of bovine tissue.

A decade and a half later, the replacement valve is deteriorating fast, and his heart is ever less efficient at pumping blood. Once a self-described "crazy hot-dog skier" and a devotee since childhood of Florida Gators football, he is growing weaker and feeling more pain.

His doctors at the Denver Health Medical Center say he will probably die within six months.

"They said that the only way to take care of this is to rip me open again, and that's not what I'm going to do," he said in the apartment he shares here with his cat.

If a less daunting treatment were available, he might try it, Mr. Mitton said. But he was told he does not qualify for newer, less invasive surgical methods. As his ability to work fades, he is also desperately worried about money and says he would choose to die rather than enter a shelter or even a hospice.

His younger sister in North Carolina, Holly Mitton-Cowan, said by telephone, "I'm trying not to cry, but I respect his decision."

Mr. Mitton is exploring the international underground market for pentobarbital, a drug used in executions and animal euthanasia. In the past, patients have obtained it by mail order or in person in Latin America or China. But the drug has become scarce, and governments have cracked down on illicit trade.

If he can get some liquid pentobarbital, Mr. Mitton said, when the time is right he will sit in his easy chair and mix it into a salty dog — a vodka, grapefruit juice and salt cocktail that was his first drink as a teenager.

If not, he said, he may resort to what some call a "chemical suicide," mixing household chemicals to produce a deadly cloud of hydrogen sulfide gas and leaving behind a toxic mess. He is also pondering a heroin overdose.

Whatever the means, he said, "I think it's best if I'm by myself. That way, nobody could get into trouble."

Doctor Loses License Over Assisted Suicides

BY ALAN BLINDER | DEC. 30, 2014

MARYLAND REGULATORS this month revoked the medical license of an anesthesiologist for helping six ill people, none of whom had terminal conditions, to commit suicide.

The doctor, Lawrence D. Egbert, 87, lost the Maryland medical license he had held for more than 60 years after a disciplinary panel for the Maryland Board of Physicians found that he had engaged in "unprofessional conduct" while working as the medical director for the Final Exit Network, which offers aid to people "who are suffering from intolerable medical circumstances."

State regulators said that Dr. Egbert had acted as what the network calls an exit guide for six people in Maryland from May 2004 to November 2008.

"Dr. Egbert reviewed their applications and medical records and recommended accepting them as members," said the order, which was signed by Christine A. Farrelly, the executive director of the Board of Physicians. "Dr. Egbert attended their suicide rehearsals. He held each member's hand and talked to him or her."

Each of the patients died, the state said, of asphyxiation caused by helium inhalation, and Dr. Egbert "removed the hoods and helium tanks" from the places where the five women and one man died. Those patients had been diagnosed with conditions that included Parkinson's disease, multiple sclerosis and chronic obstructive pulmonary disease.

In a brief telephone interview on Tuesday evening, Dr. Egbert said he planned to appeal the board's decision.

"What we're doing should be available to any patient with an incurable, horrible disease that they've tried everything on, and it doesn't seem to work," he said.

The state, he said, "misportrayed me" and was undermining what he defends as a constitutional right to "advise" people how to die.

In its order on Dec. 12, the Board of Physicians outlined four reasons it had deemed Dr. Egbert's conduct unprofessional. The board said he had violated the American Medical Association's Code of Medical Ethics and that his activities were "illegal under Maryland law." It is unclear whether Dr. Egbert will be prosecuted in Maryland.

Maryland regulators first charged Dr. Egbert with misconduct in late 2012, and an administrative law judge recommended more than a year later that he lose his medical license. Maryland records show that Dr. Egbert has not been disciplined within the last decade by other state medical boards.

The decision in Maryland is the latest effort by government agencies to sanction Dr. Egbert for his activities. Before he could stand trial in Georgia, the state's Supreme Court voted to strike down the law under which he was being prosecuted. He was acquitted of criminal charges in Arizona. He is also facing prosecution in Minnesota.

Dr. Egbert has been loosely compared to Dr. Jack Kevorkian, the Michigan pathologist who in 1998 was videotaped administering a lethal cocktail to a 52-year-old man.

"We kind of look upon him like we do Dr. Kevorkian: one of the pioneers of all of this who helped bring attention to the movement," said Dr. Frank Kavanaugh, an advisory board member for Final Exit Network.

"I think that there are some people who do it quietly," Dr. Kavanaugh added. "He always spoke out. He was always a bit of a pioneer and a rebel."

Stigma Around Physician-Assisted Dying Lingers

BY CLYDE HABERMAN | MARCH 22, 2015

"DEATH IS NOTHING at all," the English theologian Henry Scott Holland wrote a century ago in a reflection that is often quoted at funerals. Death is but life extended, Holland said: "I have only slipped away to the next room. Nothing has happened. Everything remains exactly as it was."

The words are as haunting today as they must have been in 1910 when Holland delivered them in a sermon. But in the realms of politics, medical ethics, religion and technological innovation, the reality is that death is far, very far, from nothing at all. It is the source of challenging legal and moral questions, perhaps none more searing than whether doctors ought to be permitted to usher incurably ill patients into that next room. Should they be able to help sufferers end their lives by supplying medication that would make looming death come faster?

Five states, in various forms, countenance doctor-assisted dying. Others are considering it. In California, legislation to permit such assistance is scheduled to receive a hearing this week. A lawsuit in New York that seeks a similar result was filed in State Supreme Court last month by a group of doctors and dying patients. The emotional wallop of these issues is self-evident, and it is captured in the latest installment of Retro Report, a series of video documentaries that explore major news stories of the past — looking back at where we have been to see where we may be headed.

Where better to start than with Dr. Jack Kevorkian, the Michigan pathologist who came to be known as Doctor Death? He claimed to have helped end the lives of at least 130 ailing people. Few Americans were neutral about Dr. Kevorkian, who died in 2011. To some, he was a force for good, a doctor who grabbed the country by the lapels and made it think hard about how to deal with the severe pain that many people endure as the end approaches. To others, though, he was a self-promoting merchant of death, ghoulishly interested in the mechanics of killing more than in palliative care for those in need of it.

To the authorities in Michigan, he was, ultimately, a criminal. He spent eight years in prison on a second-degree murder conviction after he had erased the thin, yet legally indelible, line separating assisted suicide from euthanasia. No longer content with merely providing patients with the means to take their own lives, the doctor did the deed himself, on national television no less.

Euthanasia is not permitted anywhere in the United States. Direct action by a doctor to take a life is deemed a step too far even by states that have no problem with indirect action: letting physicians prescribe pills that patients themselves then swallow. Are these distinctions without significant difference? Dr. Kevorkian believed so. It is the sort of question that lawmakers and judges, too, are called on to answer. Those who brought the New York lawsuit argue that equal-protection rights are violated by an existing state ban on doctor-assisted suicide (or "aid in dying," as its advocates prefer). How is it, the plaintiffs effectively ask, that doctors in New York are allowed to hasten death for some terminally ill patients by removing life support but are prohibited from hastening it for others by way of a prescription?

Arguments, pro and con, have not changed much over the years. Assisted dying was and is anathema to many religious leaders, notably in the Roman Catholic Church. For the American Medical Association, it remains "fundamentally incompatible with the physician's role as healer."

Some opponents express slippery-slope concerns: that certain patients might feel they owe it to their overburdened families to call it quits. That the poor and the uninsured, disproportionately, will have their lives cut short. That medication might be prescribed for the mentally incompetent. That doctors might move too readily to bring an end to those in the throes of depression. "We should address what would give them purpose, not give them a handful of pills," Dr. Ezekiel Emanuel, a prominent oncologist and medical ethicist, told Retro Report.

But to those in the other camp, the slippery-slope arguments are overwrought. Citing available information from the few jurisdictions where assisted dying is permitted, supporters of "dying with dignity" laws say that those looking for an early exit tend to be relatively well off and well educated. There is no evidence, they say, to suggest that such laws have been used promiscuously by either patients or their doctors. As for the medical association's ethical judgment, it "focuses too much on the physician, and not enough on the patient," said Dr. Marcia Angell, a former executive editor of The New England Journal of Medicine. Writing in The New York Review of Books in 2012, Dr. Angell asked, "Why should anyone — the state, the medical profession, or anyone else — presume to tell someone else how much suffering they must endure as their life is ending?"

In this country, Oregon has the most experience with this issue. Its voters endorsed doctor-assisted death in a 1994 referendum and again in late 1997 after the United States Supreme Court ruled unanimously that year that there is no constitutional right to die and that this is a matter for the states to decide. Washington State voters followed Oregon's lead in 2008. A year later, assisted dying was made possible in Montana by a State Supreme Court decision. In 2013, the Vermont Legislature gave its blessing, and last year so did a District Court judge in New Mexico, a ruling now under appeal.

The Oregon model is widely invoked. To obtain death-inducing medication, a patient must have a terminal illness, with no expectation of living beyond six more months. Two doctors have to attest to that. The patient must also be judged mentally competent, must be able to swallow the drugs and must be the one to ask for them — twice verbally, with each request separated by at least 15 days. Any physician unwilling to take part in this does not have to.

In Oregon's 17 years of experience with these procedures, starting in 1998, the numbers have steadily risen. There were 24 prescriptions for lethal drugs in 1998. The 2014 figure was 155, according to the state's Public Health Division. Many people who ask for the medication — typically, one-third — do not use it, for whatever reason. Of the 155 who received prescriptions last year, only 105 died from ingesting the drugs. Presumably, many of the other 50 died as well, just not from medication.

In all, across the 17 years, 1,327 Oregonians received these drugs, and 859 died from taking them. That toll amounts to less than two-tenths of 1 percent of the nearly 530,000 people who died in Oregon during that period. It hardly suggests that assisted death is rampant. But numbers go only so far in the ethical, religious and legal anguishing inherent in so grave a matter.

Those advocating a state-sanctioned right to die, like the group Compassion and Choices, say momentum is on their side, but it may be too soon to tell. And Henry Scott Holland's musings, stirring though they are, are unlikely to be much of a guide. "Life means all that it ever meant," he said. "It is the same as it ever was."

In America's juridical and political precincts, it is uncertain if that sentiment still holds true.

Lawsuit Seeks to Legalize Doctor-Assisted Suicide for Terminally Ill Patients in New York

BY ANEMONA HARTOCOLLIS | FEB. 3, 2015

A GROUP OF DOCTORS and terminally ill patients are asking New York courts to declare that doctor-assisted suicide is legal and not covered by the state's prohibition on helping people take their own lives.

Under longtime interpretations of state law, a doctor who helps a terminally ill patient die by providing a fatal dose of medication can be prosecuted under the manslaughter statute, which covers anyone who "intentionally causes or aids another person to commit suicide."

The lawsuit, to be filed Wednesday in State Supreme Court in Manhattan, contends that the law was intended to prevent someone from, for instance, helping a lovesick teenager commit suicide, but not to stop a doctor from helping a mentally competent, terminally ill patient die.

The plaintiffs also argue that because doctors are already allowed to help terminally ill patients die in some circumstances, such as when they remove life support, the fact that they cannot hasten death for other terminally ill patients violates the equal protection clause of the State Constitution.

"What we will be helping the court to see is there are many instances where patients under existing law in medicine can invite medical conduct which precipitates death," Kathryn L. Tucker, lead counsel in the case and executive director for the Disability Rights Legal Center, said this week. "Yet it is somewhat random whether any given patient will fall into that category."

Assisted suicide — advocates prefer the term "aid in dying" — is legal in only a few states, including Montana, Washington, New Mexico, Oregon and Vermont.

Kathleen M. Gallagher, director of pro-life activities for the New York State Catholic Conference, said that while she had not seen the court papers, the conference was generally opposed to assisted suicide. "We would make the distinction — and there are longstanding distinctions which are moral and medical and legal — between letting someone die a natural death and deliberately hastening someone's death by giving them a lethal dose of drugs," Ms. Gallagher said.

Ms. Gallagher said that permitting assisted suicide would undermine the physician's role as a healer, and could eventually be used as the most financially expedient option. "It forever changes the patient-physician relationship," she said.

Samuel Gorovitz, a professor of philosophy at Syracuse University who has written extensively about biomedical ethics, said the lawsuit struck him as an effort to circumvent the law by people who thought "that is easier than changing it."

Dr. Gorovitz was part of a 1994 report on assisted suicide by the state's Task Force on Life and the Law, which decided that the law should not be changed. Still, he said that, without expressing his own opinion on the topic, it might be ripe for review because of experience with assisted suicide in other states and countries and because of advances in medicine.

The plaintiffs — three patients, four doctors, a nurse and End of Life Choices New York — are suing the state attorney general, Eric T. Schneiderman, and the district attorneys who are charged with upholding the law in Westchester, Monroe, Saratoga, Bronx and New York Counties, where the plaintiffs live and practice.

Sara Myers, one of the patients, has amyotrophic lateral sclerosis, known as Lou Gehrig's disease. She uses a wheelchair. Her arms are paralyzed, her breathing and talking are compromised, and though she can still swallow, she has to be fed.

Ms. Myers, 60, did not know precisely when she might want help dying. "The line in the sand is constantly moving," she said in an

Sara Myers, at home in Manhattan, is a plaintiff in the suit that will be filed Wednesday in State Supreme Court. Ms. Myers has Lou Gehrig's disease.

interview. But she added, "Knowing you have a choice means you don't have to use it."

One of the physician plaintiffs, Timothy E. Quill, became a pioneer in the movement when he published an article in The New England Journal of Medicine in 1991, describing how he prescribed a lethal dose of sleeping pills for a leukemia patient. A grand jury declined to indict him.

He challenged the New York law on constitutional grounds, and the case went to the United States Supreme Court, which rejected the challenge in 1997. The lawsuit to be filed Wednesday does not raise any federal issues.

Dr. Quill, who is head of palliative care at the University of Rochester Medical Center, said he recently had a patient whose bones were breaking from advanced cancer, and consciously stopped eating and drinking. "It took him about 10 days to die," Dr. Quill said. "You have to be incredibly disciplined to do it."

On the legislative front, State Senator Brad Hoylman, a Manhattan Democrat, has proposed a law that would permit doctors to prescribe lethal drugs to terminally ill patients and is seeking co-sponsors. Mr. Hoylman has said he was inspired by Brittany Maynard, 29, a California woman with terminal brain cancer who moved to Oregon so she could die under that state's law. Through videos posted on YouTube, she became a public face of the "death with dignity" movement, and died in November of an overdose of barbiturates at her home in Portland.

California Governor Signs
Assisted Suicide Bill Into Law

BY IAN LOVETT AND RICHARD PÉREZ-PEÑA | OCT. 5, 2015

LOS ANGELES — California will become the fifth state to allow doctors to prescribe life-ending drugs to terminally ill patients, after Gov. Jerry Brown signed the measure into law on Monday, ending his months of silence on one of the most emotional issues in the state this year.

In an unusually personal signing message, the governor, a former Jesuit seminarian, signaled how torn he was by the issue.

"I do not know what I would do if I were dying in prolonged and excruciating pain," he wrote. "I am certain, however, that it would be a comfort to be able to consider the options afforded by this bill. And I wouldn't deny that right to others."

The law will take effect 90 days after the special legislative session in which it was passed adjourns, which lawmakers expected would be sometime next year.

Oregon has allowed what opponents call "assisted suicide" and supporters term "aid in dying" since 1997, and, after a Supreme Court ruling in 2006 that affirmed the law, Washington, Montana and Vermont have also approved the practice.

Opponents have long raised concerns that ill and disabled people could be coerced into choosing death over more care, which can be expensive and burdensome. The Catholic Church, which considers suicide a sin, also helped lead opposition.

Dr. Aaron Kheriaty, director of the medical ethics program at the University of California, Irvine, School of Medicine, said he expected a number of hospitals would refuse to offer life-ending drugs, to preserve their own reputations and relationships with patients.

"I worry about what this is going to do to the perception of medicine," he said. "I think you're going to see more and more mistrust of medical professionals by patients worried about what will happen if they enroll in end-of-life care."

Past efforts to allow doctors to help patients end their lives in California had failed. But this year, support for more end-of-life choices was galvanized around the country by the case of Brittany Maynard, 29, a Bay Area woman who received a diagnosis of terminal brain cancer. Before she died last November, Ms. Maynard became a spokeswoman for the "death with dignity" movement, moving her family to Oregon so she could die on her own terms, and drawing national attention to her cause.

In 2014, four states considered bills to allow physicians to help terminally ill patients end their lives; this year, that number increased to 24 states plus the District of Columbia, according to Compassion and Choices, a group that supported the law.

Mickey MacIntyre, the chief program officer for Compassion and Choices, said he hoped passage in California would spur other states to pass similar measures.

"California will provide some momentum and space for legislators to see that they can enact laws that are popular, supported by law, and bring relief to those who need it at the ends of their lives," he said.

Debbie Ziegler, Ms. Maynard's mother, said news that the governor had signed the bill her family had backed was a "bittersweet moment."

"Today gives my daughter's death purpose, and I think any mother who's lost a child wants that," she said. "Californians are going to benefit from this whether they're terminally ill or not because this opens up a dialogue about death and dying. This law means that conversation is going to be more open and more candid."

The California law includes protections designed to assuage concerns about potential abuse. Patients must be terminally ill and mentally sound; they must be capable of administering the medication themselves; and two different doctors must approve it.

Hospitals and doctors will also have the option of not offering end-of-life drugs.

"We've crafted the strongest protections of any such law that currently exists," said Bill Monning, a California senator and one of the law's sponsors. He added that, despite fears by opponents, hospice care had grown extensively in Oregon since that state's "death with dignity" law was approved.

In his signing message, Mr. Brown wrote that he had seriously weighed arguments from people lobbying on both sides, and consulted with "a Catholic bishop, two of my own doctors, and former classmates and friends who take varied, contradictory and nuanced positions."

"In the end," he wrote, "I was left to reflect on what I would want in the face of my own death."

IAN LOVETT reported from Los Angeles, and RICHARD PÉREZ-PEÑA from New York.

Who May Die? California Patients and Doctors Wrestle With Assisted Suicide

BY JENNIFER MEDINA | JUNE 9, 2016

LOS ANGELES — On Thursday, California became the fourth state in the country to put in effect a law allowing assisted suicide for the terminally ill, what has come to be known as aid in dying. Lawmakers here approved the legislation last year, after Brittany Maynard, a 29-year-old schoolteacher who had brain cancer, received international attention for her decision to move to Oregon, where terminally ill patients have been allowed to take drugs to die since 1997.

Oregon was the first state to pass an assisted suicide law, and was followed by Washington and Vermont. Under a Montana court ruling, doctors cannot be prosecuted for helping terminally ill patients die, as long as the patient makes a written request. With the California law, 16 percent of the country's population has a legal option for terminally ill patients to determine the moment of their death, up from 4 percent.

In the states with assisted suicide laws, the number of people who request and take medication to hasten dying has steadily increased. In Oregon, for example, 16 people ended their lives under the law in 1998, and by 2015, that number had grown to 132.

The California legislation is strict, intended to ensure that patients have thought through the decision and are making it voluntarily. Patients must make multiple requests for the medication and have a prognosis of less than six months to live.

Many hospitals have not yet released policies for dealing with the law. And no doctor, health system or pharmacy will be required to comply with a patient's request. Doctors who object to the practice are not even required to refer patients who request the medication to another physician.

Roman Catholic and other religious health systems have said they will not participate. "We are crossing a line — from being a society

Debbie Ziegler in 2015 with a photo of her daughter, Brittany Maynard, a brain cancer patient who moved from California to Oregon to legally end her life in 2014.

that cares for those who are aging and sick to a society that kills those whose suffering we can no longer tolerate," José H. Gomez, the Catholic archbishop of Los Angeles, said in a statement Wednesday.

Here is how two patients and two doctors are preparing for the new order.

'I DON'T WANT TO BECOME A BURDEN'

Kristy Allan, 63, lives in Placerville, where her small bungalow overlooks the lush foothills of the Sierra Nevada. With her athletic frame, she does not look like someone ready to die. But she has been under hospice care since the start of the year, having already undergone four rounds of chemotherapy since learning she had Stage 4 colon cancer in 2009. She has already talked to her doctors about her desire to get the medication that will allow her to die when she chooses, and she plans to make her request formal this week. She does not know with certainty when, or even if, she will take it. But she knows what would make her ready to do so.

"I don't want to become a burden to my family. I don't want my husband to take care of certain hygienic needs. That's my nonnegotiable thing. It's a huge relief knowing it is legal. To have to take it, to go to the point where you know you are ending your life, that's hard. But I know that I could do it when it comes to that point."

Ms. Allan has already defied some predictions. When her 30-year-old daughter got engaged last spring, she wondered whether she would make it to the wedding. But she did, designing and sewing her mother-of-the-bride dress herself, and baking desserts for the reception.

Ms. Allan has spoken to her husband and her two adult children about the decision.

Kristy Allan, who lives in Placerville, Calif., has terminal cancer and wants to be able to decide when and how to die.

"They've always been in support of me. They've never asked, 'Are you sure?' or challenged me. Last year they said there was a new drug available that would maybe give me another six months, but it would mean lab work once a week and low white blood cell count. Every time you start a new chemo drug, it's really scary because you don't know how you're going to feel. I don't know how sick I'm going to feel, how little energy I'll have. I just said, 'Enough.' If there were really further curative measures, I would not be declining it, thank you very much, I would say, 'Give them to me.' But there aren't any. I wasn't going to put myself through six months of that. I knew I had six months in me. The fact is there are no curative measures. All along I was told I was not going to come out of this alive. With hospice, there are really no more tests to be done, no more treatment. It's a relief."

Wolf Breiman, 88, who learned he had multiple myeloma seven years ago, does not know what will push him to the edge to ask for the medication. But Mr. Breiman, who lives in Ventura, relishes the idea of having the right to choose precisely when and where to die.

"Whatever gives you a sense of control over your destiny is empowering. I feel assured that in the circumstances, ... I'd be able to determine what to do. ... It just absolutely makes sense, it's such a basic right to me. I don't see how you can take the Constitution seriously and not agree that it's consistent with the rest of the liberties we have."

'THIS IS NEW TERRITORY'

Dr. Sunita Puri, a palliative medicine specialist at Keck Medicine of the University of Southern California, is writing the hospital's policy on the new law. To prepare, she asked her colleagues what they would do if their patients sought help in dying. While more than 60 percent of those she surveyed said they supported the legislation in theory, half of the doctors who responded told her they would not prescribe the medication themselves.

"My sense of talking to colleagues is they simply don't know enough about what the medication will be, and part of it is not knowing if it is resulting in a comfortable experience that leads to their death. They take very

seriously the obligation to support patients and not do something harmful.
The other reason is that people feel very uncomfortable about what this act
means for the changing role of physicians in society, what would be right
for patients and what would be appropriate for them to do."

Some health care systems will make a psychiatric evaluation a prerequisite for receiving the drugs. Dr. Puri has heard from many doctors who worry that they are not fully prepared to determine whether a patient is able to make the request to die, not suffering from depression or in the kind of pain that palliative and hospice care could alleviate.

"These are not going to be simple and easy conversations. Everyone wants
what would be right for patients. The stakes are very high obviously. We
assess for capacity every day, but this is new territory. There's a difference
between questions about it and wanting to pursue it, and that is going to
require quite a bit of conversation, of back and forth between oncologists
and palliative care doctors and the patients."

JENNA SCHOENEFELD FOR THE NEW YORK TIMES

Dr. Sunita Puri, a palliative medicine specialist at Keck Medicine of the University of Southern California, is writing the hospital's policy on the new law.

In Berkeley, Dr. Lonny Shavelson bristles each time he hears a doctor talk about discomfort with prescribing end-of-life medication. A former emergency room physician, Dr. Shavelson has just begun his own practice dedicated to providing care for those seeking to end their lives. Here is how he imagines talking to reluctant doctors.

"What I've said to them is, 'Were you comfortable the first time you did chest surgery? Were you comfortable the first time you drew blood?' I don't understand when being uncomfortable became a reason not to do something in medicine. We make uncomfortable decisions all the time. When somebody says, 'I am ready to end dialysis and let myself die,' that's a momentous decision and it might make us uncomfortable. The best answer I can get is that it is a difference of mechanics. But we're agreeing that they are ready to die. It's that the mechanism seems fairly irrelevant."

Dr. Shavelson, who will charge patients $200 for an initial consultation and $1,800 if they move forward, said the most important response he would have for any patient who approached him was simple: Why? He believes the approach should not be different from any other aspect of medicine.

"We always listen to the patient. We never tell a patient: 'This is what you have to do. You have no choice.' Yet at the moment when their life is ending — when they say, 'I don't want to live in this bed for the next three weeks waiting to die' — it's an odd change in the consent procedure. Suddenly they become wrong and we become right. That does not make sense to me. Dying should not be completely separate from everything else we do in medicine."

Assisted Suicide Study Questions Its Use for Mentally Ill

BY BENEDICT CAREY | FEB. 10, 2016

A NEW STUDY of doctor-assisted death for people with mental disorders raises questions about the practice, finding that in more than half of approved cases, people declined treatment that could have helped, and that many cited loneliness as an important reason for wanting to die. The study, of cases in the Netherlands, should raise concerns for other countries debating where to draw the line when it comes to people's right to die, experts said.

At least three countries — the Netherlands, Belgium and Switzerland — allow assisted suicides for people who have severe psychiatric problems and others, like Canada, are debating such measures, citing the rights of people with untreatable mental illness. Laws in the United States, passed in five states, restrict doctor-assisted suicide to mentally competent adults with terminal illnesses only, not for disorders like depression and schizophrenia.

The study, published Wednesday in the journal JAMA Psychiatry, finds that cases of doctor-assisted death for psychiatric reasons were not at all clear-cut, even in the Netherlands, the country with the longest tradition of carefully evaluating such end-of-life choices. People who got assistance to die often sought help from doctors they had not seen before, and many used what the study called a "mobile end-of-life clinic" — a nurse and a doctor, funded by a local euthanasia advocacy organization.

"The criteria in the Netherlands essentially require that the person's disorder be intractable and untreatable, and this study shows that evaluating each of those elements turns out to be problematic," said Dr. Paul S. Appelbaum, a professor of psychiatry, medicine and law at Columbia University.

Dr. Appelbaum added, "The idea that people are leaving their treating physician and going to a clinic that exists solely for this purpose,

Dr. Scott Y. H. Kim, a psychiatrist and bioethicist at the National Institutes of Health, led a study of cases of doctor-assisted death for psychiatric distress in the Netherlands.

and being evaluated not by a psychiatrist but by someone else who has to make these very difficult decisions about levels of suffering and disease — it seems to me like the worst possible way of implementing this process."

The study, led by Dr. Scott Y. H. Kim, a psychiatrist and bioethicist at the National Institutes of Health, looked at records of most of the cases of doctor-assisted death for psychiatric distress from 2011 to mid-2014. In 37 of those 66 cases, people had refused a recommended treatment that could have helped. The study did not evaluate cases of people who had been denied assistance.

Depression was the most common diagnosis, but loneliness was also a frequent theme. "The patient was an utterly lonely man whose life had been a failure," read one account. In another, a woman in her 70s said she and her husband had decided years earlier that they would not live without each other. She had no health problems, but after her husband died, she described her life as "a living hell."

Five states in this country have laws allowing doctors to prescribe life-ending drugs to mentally competent, terminally ill adults: Oregon, Vermont, Montana, Washington, and California. The California law is expected to take effect this year. By contrast, laws in several European countries allow such assistance for any competent person with "unbearable suffering" — regardless of the cause.

Last year, a team of doctors in Belgium, where laws are similar to those in the Netherlands, reported that most people who sought doctor-assisted death for psychiatric problems had depression, personality disorders or both. The new study of the Netherlands fills out that picture considerably, detailing the agonizing decisions by both doctors and patients in cases that went forward, ending in voluntary death.

The researchers, who included Dr. John Peteet of Harvard Medical School and Raymond De Vries of the University of Michigan and Maastricht University in the Netherlands, found that 46 of the patients had been women, most 60 or older.

The depression was often mixed with other problems, like substance abuse, mild dementia or physical pain. More than half had received a diagnosis of a personality disorder, like avoidant or dependent personality, which are typically bound up with relationship problems. The group also included people with diagnoses of eating disorders and autism spectrum conditions. Many reported being intensely lonely.

"The Dutch system is really the idealized setting in which to try something like this," said Dr. Kim, in an interview. "But still, you can see that there are many cases that make us question whether this is the right practice."

In the Dutch system, consulting doctors review petitions for assistance in dying. In one quarter of the cases, the study found, the doctors disagreed.

Barbara Coombs Lee, president of Compassion and Choices, which advocates compassionate end-of-life care, said the debate over people with psychiatric conditions was not relevant to laws in the United States, which have been modeled on Oregon's 1997 Death With Dignity Act.

"I have seen no parallel movement or discussion at any level in this country," Ms. Coombs Lee said. "I don't know of anyone ever proposing this here, or of any poll supporting anything but self-administration by mentally competent, terminally ill adults."

Physician Aid in Dying Gains Acceptance in the U.S.

BY PAULA SPAN | JAN. 16, 2017

JUDITH KATHERINE DUNNING had been waiting anxiously for California to adopt legislation that would make it legal for her to end her life.

The cancer in her brain was progressing despite several rounds of treatment. At 68, she spent most of her day asleep and needed an aide to help with basic tasks.

More centrally, Ms. Dunning — who, poignantly, had worked as an oral historian in Berkeley, Calif. — was losing her ability to speak. Even before the End of Life Option Act became law, in October 2015, she had recorded a video expressing her desire to hasten her death.

The video, she hoped, would make her wishes clear, in case there were any doubts later on.

"She felt she had completed all the important tasks of her life," recalled her physician, Dr. Michael Rabow, director of the symptom management service at the University of California, San Francisco. "When she could no longer communicate, life was no longer worth living."

In recent months, this option has become available to a growing number of Americans. Last June, aid-in-dying legislation took effect in California, the most populous state. In November, Colorado voters approved a ballot measure by nearly a two-thirds majority. The District of Columbia Council has passed a similar law, and the mayor quietly signed it last month.

Aid in dying was already legal in Washington, Vermont, Montana and Oregon. So even if the District of Columbia's law is blocked, as a prominent Republican representative has threatened to do, the country has arrived at a remarkable moment: Close to 20 percent of Americans live in jurisdictions where adults can legally end their lives if they are terminally ill and meet eligibility requirements.

DAVID PLUNKERT

The laws, all based on the Death With Dignity Act Oregon adopted in 1997, allow physicians to write prescriptions for lethal drugs when patients qualify. The somewhat complicated procedure involves two oral requests and a written one, extensive discussions, and approval by two physicians. Patients must have the mental capacity to make medical decisions.

While that process took shape in Oregon two decades ago, the cultural and political context surrounding it has changed considerably. The states recently considering the issue differ from earlier adopters, and as opposition from some longtime adversaries has softened, new obstacles have arisen.

Historically, aid in dying has generated fierce resistance from the Catholic Church, from certain disability-rights activists, and from others who cite religious or moral objections. Even the terminology — aid in dying? assisted suicide? death with dignity? — creates controversy. But the concept has long drawn broad support in public opinion polls.

Polltakers for the General Social Survey, done by NORC at the University of Chicago have asked a representative national sample this question since 1977: "When a person has a disease that cannot be cured, do you think doctors should be allowed by law to end the patient's life by some painless means if the patient and his family request it?"

The proportion of Americans responding affirmatively, always a substantial majority, has bounced between 66 and 69 percent for 15 years. But support was not evenly distributed: Such laws initially were enacted in states with predominantly white populations like Oregon, and to date the vast majority of patients who have used them are white.

"I hear people talk all the time about this being a rich white person's issue," said Donna Smith, legislative manager for the District of Columbia at the group Compassion and Choices, who is African-American. "Now, we have proof on the ground that that is not true."

Indeed, aid in dying has expanded to more diverse locales. Non-Hispanic whites represent a minority of Californians. Colorado is more than 21 percent Latino. In the District of Columbia, nearly half of whose residents are African-American, five of six black council members voted in favor of the legislation.

State medical societies, once active foes of aid-in-dying initiatives, also have begun shifting their positions, citing deep divisions among their members. The California Medical Association, the Colorado Medical Society and the Medical Society of the District of Columbia all took officially neutral stances as legislators and voters debated, depriving opponents of influential allies. So has the state medical society in Maryland, where legislators plan to reintroduce a bill (the third attempt) this month.

The American Medical Association, an opponent since 1993, has asked its Council on Ethical and Judicial Affairs to look at the aid-in-dying issue and submit a report in June, though without recommending any policy.

But even as the idea gains acceptance, passage of a bill or ballot measure does not always make aid in dying broadly available to those who want it. In addition to the safeguards the law requires, its practice can be balky — at least in the early stages.

State opt-out provisions allow any individual or institution to decline to provide prescriptions. In California, Catholic health care systems have opted out, predictably, but so have a number of others, including Vitas, the nation's largest hospice chain.

Moreover, California hospitals and hospices can forbid their affiliated physicians to write the necessary prescriptions, even if they are acting privately. Some health systems with hundreds of doctors have done so. (Vermont, Colorado and the District of Columbia allow doctors to make individual decisions.)

"The shortage of participating providers has led to a lot of patient and family frustration," said Dr. Laura Petrillo, palliative care physician at the San Francisco V.A. Medical Center, in an email.

"They had the expectation that it would be available and happen seamlessly once the law went into effect, and then find themselves needing to do a lot of legwork" to find doctors willing to prescribe lethal drugs and pharmacies to fill prescriptions, she said.

Sometimes, when patients have waited until late in their illnesses, they die before they can become eligible for assisted death. Or they become too physically or mentally incapacitated to take the drugs themselves, as legally required, even if they do qualify.

In areas where many providers opt out, very sick patients may have to travel long distances to use the law. And costs can also prove a barrier.

Some private insurers pay for the necessary doctors' visits and drugs. In California, most do, said Matt Whitaker, state director of Compassion and Choices, the leading aid-in-dying advocacy group. But Congress has long prohibited the use of federal dollars for aid in dying, so Medicare and the Department of Veterans Affairs will not cover it. States like California and Oregon have agreed to cover the costs for Medicaid recipients; others do not.

Cost mattered less years ago, when a lethal dose of barbiturates ran a couple of hundred dollars. But in 2015, as California legislators introduced their bill, Valeant Pharmaceuticals acquired Seconal, the most commonly used aid-in-dying drug. The company, known (and condemned) for a similar strategy with other medications, spiked the price, a move Mr. Whitaker called "ethically and morally bankrupt."

Now, patients whose insurers will not cover aid in dying face paying $3,000 to $4,000 for the drug. Valeant has denied the suggestion that it was exploiting the new law. As a result, physicians are turning to alternative — and less-well-understood — combinations of opioids and sedatives for those who cannot afford the standard medication.

Despite such obstacles and disappointments, an emboldened Compassion and Choices, with a staff that has tripled since 2008 and an annual budget that has nearly quadrupled to $16.9 million — is eyeing its next targets. Over several years, its leaders think they can help legalize aid in dying in Maryland, Hawaii and New York.

Aid in dying, it should be noted, may be a vehemently debated issue, with campaigns that can involve thousands of participants and millions of dollars — but it ultimately has affected a tiny proportion of people.

The number of residents taking advantage of these laws in Oregon and Washington has climbed in the past two years. Still, after nearly 20 years in Oregon and eight in Washington, far fewer than 1 percent of annual deaths involve a lethal prescription. (Of those residents who do receive one, about a third do not use it.) It's not the way most Americans choose to die, even when they have the legal option.

Yet the end of life care most people receive needs substantial improvement. While partisans fight over aid in dying, skeptics like Dr. Rabow note, the complicated and expensive measures that could improve end-of-life care for the great majority — overhauled medical education, better staffed and operated nursing homes, increased access to hospice and palliative care — go largely unaddressed.

Still, Ms. Dunning was Dr. Rabow's longtime patient. When California's act took effect, she began the process of requesting lethal medication. Her speech had slurred further, but not yet enough to render her unintelligible.

Dr. Rabow did not want to see her die, and he is no fan of the aid-in-dying movement. But Ms. Dunning had been clear, consistent and determined. He wrote the prescription.

"She was ready to have her life end, and no amount of support or medication or counseling would change the situation," he said.

In September, she invited him to her home, where she planned to swallow the fatal slurry of barbiturates. On the appointed day, Dr. Rabow arrived to find "a house full of people who didn't want her to end her life, but were there to support her and respect her well-considered decision."

Over the course of the day, people said their goodbyes, then withdrew to leave Ms. Dunning with her closest relatives, her hospice nurse and her doctor. Her son mixed her Seconal solution and she swallowed it, no simple task for someone with advanced cancer.

She lost consciousness almost immediately and died several hours later.

"I wished she could have had a natural life span," Dr. Rabow said. "And I would have made a different choice. But I was honored to be there to watch this very dignified woman live her life the way she wanted to."

Gorsuch Staunchly Opposes 'Aid in Dying.' Does It Matter?

BY PAULA SPAN | FEB. 24, 2017

EVER SINCE PRESIDENT TRUMP nominated Judge Neil M. Gorsuch to fill the empty seat on the Supreme Court, interested parties have been combing through his writings and appellate court rulings looking for signs and portents.

If he's confirmed, how might Judge Gorsuch vote on affirmative action questions? Or challenges to Roe v. Wade?

But nobody has to do much head-scratching over his position on medical aid in dying. In 2006, the year he was appointed to the federal Court of Appeals in Denver, Princeton University Press published Judge Gorsuch's book, "The Future of Assisted Suicide and Euthanasia."

It leaves little room for doubt. Over 226 pages (in paperback), Judge Gorsuch pursues a legal and philosophical argument that "assisted suicide and euthanasia" should be outlawed because "all human life is fundamentally and inherently valuable" and "the intentional taking of human life by private persons is always wrong."

In Oregon, the first state to legalize aid in dying, the handful of patients using the law had been white and well educated, the author noted in an epilogue, leading him to wonder "whether assisted suicide is a matter of necessity or more of a lifestyle choice by people who have always tended to control their lives and now wish to control their death."

(Even the terminology is perilous. The phrase "assisted suicide," now used mostly by opponents, tends to signal disapproval. For a while, supporters preferred "death with dignity." At least "aid in dying" doesn't imply that those who die without lethal prescriptions lack dignity.)

Judge Gorsuch's position is creating anxiety in a movement that recently celebrated victories in several states and expressed optimism about winning more. "He has revealed tremendous personal hostility," said Kathryn Tucker, executive director of the End of Life Liberty Project.

"I can't think of any other justice who has written so much on the subject or is so opposed," said Kevin Diaz, legal director of the advocacy group Compassion & Choices.

As an Antonin Scalia-style originalist, Judge Gorsuch presumably would find constitutional only those rights actually addressed in the Constitution or determined to be in the framers' minds when they wrote it. Neither the document nor its authors had anything to say about a right to hasten one's death with lethal medication when terminally ill.

Yet supporters of aid in dying don't sound as despondent as one might expect, even if Judge Gorsuch is confirmed. Why? They don't see the issue coming before the Supreme Court anytime soon.

The court has already weighed in, twice. In 1997, the justices heard combined cases from Washington State and New York brought by doctors and dying patients who claimed a constitutional right to physician-assisted death — and ruled unanimously against them.

"This is not an area of law with a sharp liberal-conservative divide," said Michael Dorf, a constitutional law professor at Cornell University. "Even the liberal justices rejected the argument that there's any constitutional right to physician aid in dying."

But the ruling didn't prohibit — and even seemed to encourage — individual state efforts to wrestle with the question. As Chief Justice William H. Rehnquist wrote, the decision "permits this debate to continue, as it should in a democratic society."

Oregon enacted its Death With Dignity law that year. The Bush administration tried to block it by depriving participating doctors of their federal licenses to prescribe controlled substances, but the Supreme Court slapped down that argument, 6 to 3.

Five other states (Washington, Montana, Vermont, California and Colorado) and the District of Columbia have since legalized aid

Judge Neil Gorsuch, President Trump's nominee for the Supreme Court, met with Senator Chris Murphy of Connecticut in his office on Capitol Hill on Feb. 16, 2017.

in dying through legislation, referendums or court cases. And state courts are where the legal action is likely to remain.

"Proponents of aid in dying, like proponents of other progressive views of the Constitution, are going to stay the heck out of the U.S. Supreme Court," said Vincent Bonventre, a constitutional law professor at Albany Law School in New York.

"They have a much, much better chance of getting aid in dying recognized as a protected right by going to some state supreme courts around the country."

One area where Judge Gorsuch might have influence, Mr. Diaz said, is in religious-exemption cases. As an appellate court judge hearing the Hobby Lobby case, Judge Gorsuch argued in a concurring opinion that employers with religious objections could decline to cover contraception as part of workers' health insurance. The Supreme Court later agreed.

In Vermont, two medical groups have challenged the state's aid-in-dying law, saying that if doctors decline to participate on religious grounds, they should not have to refer patients to other providers or mention the option at all.

Because it's being heard in a federal court, Mr. Diaz said, that case could eventually reach the Supreme Court. But even a decision for the plaintiffs wouldn't overturn aid-in-dying laws altogether.

As a practical matter, groups advocating the cause find themselves in state courts almost continually. Montana residents can seek lethal prescriptions at the end of life because the state's Supreme Court ruled in 2009 that no state statute outlawed it; New Mexicans have no such legal option, after that state's Supreme Court last year declined to find aid in dying constitutionally protected.

(A newly enacted District of Columbia aid-in-dying law stands for now. Congress adjourned this month without approving the resolution that would have blocked it.)

Supporters often fight rear-guard legal actions. In California, for example, groups have sued in state court to stop the new End of Life Option Act, which took effect in June.

In other states, though, it's supporters of aid in dying who turn to the courts. In Massachusetts and Hawaii, physicians and patients have filed suits arguing that (as in Montana) the practice is not outlawed by state statute and should be legal.

In 2015, New York patients and physicians brought the Myers case, named for a Manhattan resident, Sara Myers, who had amyotrophic lateral sclerosis, or Lou Gehrig's disease.

Lower courts dismissed the suit, but the Court of Appeals, the state's highest, has agreed to hear arguments, expected this spring. (Ms. Myers has died in the meantime.)

Should the New York court — or any state high court — find aid in dying protected under its state constitution, it won't matter who sits on the Supreme Court.

"The Supreme Court doesn't have the right to review that," because it doesn't involve interpretation of the federal Constitution, said Mr. Dorf, who has worked on an amicus brief in the Myers case on behalf of law professors. "New York is the final arbiter."

New York's highest court has national clout, said Edward Mechmann, a lawyer who is also filing an amicus brief in the case as public policy director for the Archdiocese of New York. If the justices were to find aid in dying legal, "I think it would be very influential, judicially and legislatively," he said.

It is not impossible that an aid-in-dying case could wend its way to the Supreme Court, Mr. Bonventre pointed out. It might involve a patient or doctor in a military hospital or other federal installation, for instance. In that case, Judge Gorsuch could have considerable impact. (Mr. Diaz argues that having denounced the practice in his book, Judge Gorsuch should recuse himself.)

Years hence, if additional states have adopted aid-in-dying laws and the Supreme Court looks more hospitable, advocates might actually want to bring a federal case that could establish constitutional protection in every state.

But for now, said Ms. Tucker, lead counsel in the Myers case, "citizens nationwide who care about individual liberty — reproductive rights, gay rights, end of life — need to look to state high courts to be their guardians."

CHAPTER 3

Personal Stories

Ultimately the decision to end one's own life is a highly personal one that many feel overrides any question of legality or ethics. In this chapter's articles, the lives of individuals who have made the choice to end their lives through physician-assisted suicide are documented by reporters, obituary writers and family members. What emerges is a nuanced look at the factors that contribute to the decision to end a life.

With Help, Conductor and Wife Ended Lives

BY JOHN F. BURNS | JULY 14, 2009

LONDON — The controversy over the ethical and legal issues surrounding assisted suicide for the terminally ill was thrown into stark relief on Tuesday with the announcement that one of Britain's most distinguished orchestra conductors, Sir Edward Downes, had flown to Switzerland last week with his wife and joined her in drinking a lethal cocktail of barbiturates provided by an assisted-suicide clinic.

Although friends who spoke to the British news media said Sir Edward was not known to have been terminally ill, they said he wanted to die with his ailing wife, who had been his partner for more than half a century.

The couple's children said in an interview with The London Evening Standard that on Tuesday of last week they accompanied their father, 85, and their mother, Joan, 74, on the flight to Zurich, where the Swiss group Dignitas helped arrange the suicides. On Friday, the children said, they watched, weeping, as their parents drank "a small quantity of clear liquid" before lying down on adjacent beds, holding hands.

"Within a couple of minutes they were asleep, and died within 10 minutes," Caractacus Downes, the couple's 41-year-old son, said in the interview after his return to Britain. "They wanted to be next to each other when they died." He added, "It is a very civilized way to end your life, and I don't understand why the legal position in this country doesn't allow it."

Sir Edward, who was described in a statement issued earlier on Tuesday by Mr. Downes and his sister, Boudicca, 39, as "almost blind and increasingly deaf," was principal conductor of the BBC Philharmonic Orchestra from 1980 to 1991. He was also a conductor of the Royal Opera House at Covent Garden in London, where he led 950 performances over more than 50 years.

Lady Downes, who British newspapers said was in the final stages of terminal cancer, was a former ballet dancer, choreographer and television producer who devoted her later years to working as her husband's assistant.

"After 54 happy years together, they decided to end their own lives rather than continue to struggle with serious health problems," the Downes children said in their statement.

British families who have used the Zurich clinic in the past have said that Dignitas charges about $6,570 for each assisted suicide.

Scotland Yard said in a statement on Tuesday that it had been informed on Monday "that a man and a woman" from London had died in Switzerland, and that it was "looking into the circumstances." The information that prompted the police inquiry appeared to have been given voluntarily by the Downes family, which, Caractacus Downes said, "didn't want to be untruthful about what had happened."

"Even if they arrest us and send us to prison, it would have made no difference because it is what our parents wanted," he said.

Attempting suicide has not been a criminal offense in Britain since

1961, but assisting others to kill themselves is. But since the Zurich clinic run by Dignitas was established in 1998 under Swiss laws that allow clinics to provide lethal drugs, British authorities have effectively turned a blind eye to Britons who go there to die.

None of the family members and friends who have accompanied the 117 people living in Britain who have traveled to the Zurich clinic for help in ending their lives have been charged with an offense. Legal experts said it was unlikely that that would change in the Downes case.

But British news reports about the Downeses' suicides noted one factor that appeared to set the case apart from others involving the Dignitas clinic: Sir Edward appeared not to have been terminally ill. There have been at least three other cases similar to the Downeses', in which a spouse who was not terminally ill chose to die with the other.

Sir Edward was known for his support for British composers and his passion for Prokofiev and Verdi. After studying at the Royal College of Music in London, he joined the Royal Opera House in 1952. His first assignment was prompting the soprano Maria Callas. He traveled widely as a conductor and became music director of the Australian Opera in the 1970s.

Friends of Sir Edward said that his decision to die with his wife did not surprise them. "Ted was completely rational," said Richard Wigley, the general manager of the BBC Philharmonic. "So I can well imagine him, being so rational, saying, 'It's been great, so let's end our lives together.' "

Jonathan Groves, Sir Edward's manager, called their decision "typically brave and courageous."

But even among those who support decriminalizing assisted suicide, Sir Edward's death raised troubling questions. Sarah Wootton, chief executive of Dignity in Dying, said in a BBC interview that the growing numbers of Britons going abroad to die, and the manner of their deaths, made it more urgent to amend Britain's laws. There are "no safeguards, no brakes on the process at all," she said.

The British Medical Association voted this month against legalizing assisted suicide, or lifting the threat of prosecution from "friends and relatives who accompany loved ones to die abroad." Last week, the House of Lords defeated a bill that would have allowed people, subject to safeguards, to travel abroad to help people choosing to die.

In Ill Doctor, a Surprise Reflection of Who Picks Assisted Suicide

BY KATIE HAFNER | AUG. 11, 2012

SEATTLE — Dr. Richard Wesley has amyotrophic lateral sclerosis, the incurable disease that lays waste to muscles while leaving the mind intact. He lives with the knowledge that an untimely death is chasing him down, but takes solace in knowing that he can decide exactly when, where and how he will die.

Under Washington State's Death With Dignity Act, his physician has given him a prescription for a lethal dose of barbiturates. He would prefer to die naturally, but if dying becomes protracted and difficult, he plans to take the drugs and die peacefully within minutes.

"It's like the definition of pornography," Dr. Wesley, 67, said at his home here in Seattle, with Mount Rainier in the distance. "I'll know it's time to go when I see it."

Washington followed Oregon in allowing terminally ill patients to get a prescription for drugs that will hasten death. Critics of such laws feared that poor people would be pressured to kill themselves because they or their families could not afford end-of-life care. But the demographics of patients who have gotten the prescriptions are surprisingly different than expected, according to data collected by Oregon and Washington through 2011.

Dr. Wesley is emblematic of those who have taken advantage of the law. They are overwhelmingly white, well educated and financially comfortable. And they are making the choice not because they are in pain but because they want to have the same control over their deaths that they have had over their lives.

While preparing advance medical directives and choosing hospice and palliative care over aggressive treatment have become mainstream options, physician-assisted dying remains taboo for many people. Voters in Massachusetts will consider a ballot initiative in

Dr. Richard Wesley, who received a diagnosis of Lou Gehrig's disease in 2008, at home with his wife and two of his children.

November on a law nearly identical to those in the Pacific Northwest, but high-profile legalization efforts have failed in California, Hawaii and Maine.

Oregon put its Death With Dignity Act in place in 1997, and Washington's law went into effect in 2009. Some officials worried that thousands of people would migrate to both states for the drugs.

"There was a lot of fear that the elderly would be lined up in their R.V.'s at the Oregon border," said Barbara Glidewell, an assistant professor at Oregon Health and Science University.

That has not happened, although the number of people who have taken advantage of the law has risen over time. In the first years, Oregon residents who died using drugs they received under the law accounted for one in 1,000 deaths. The number is now roughly one in 500 deaths. At least 596 Oregonians have died that way since 1997. In Washington, 157 such deaths have been reported, roughly one in 1,000.

In Oregon, the number of men and women who have died that way is roughly equal, and their median age is 71. Eighty-one percent have had cancer, and 7 percent A.L.S., which is also known as Lou Gehrig's disease. The rest have had a variety of illnesses, including lung and heart disease. The statistics are similar in Washington.

There were fears of a "slippery slope" — that the law would gradually expand to include those with nonterminal illnesses or that it would permit physicians to take a more active role in the dying process itself. But those worries have not been borne out, experts say.

Dr. Wesley, a pulmonologist and critical care physician, voted for the initiative when it was on the ballot in 2008, two years after he retired. "All my career, I believed that whatever makes people comfortable at the end of their lives is their own choice to make," he said.

But Dr. Wesley had no idea that his vote would soon become intensely personal.

In the months before the vote, he started having trouble lifting weights in the gym. He also noticed a hollow between his left thumb and index finger where muscle should be. A month after casting his vote, he received a diagnosis of A.L.S. Patients with the disease typically live no more than four years after the onset of symptoms, but the amount of time left to them can vary widely.

In the summer of 2010, after a bout of pneumonia and with doctors agreeing that he most likely had only six months to live, Dr. Wesley got his prescription for barbiturates. But he has not used them, and the progression of his disease has slowed, although he now sits in a wheelchair that he cannot operate. He has lost the use of his limbs and, as the muscles around his lungs weaken, he relies increasingly on a respirator. His speech is clear, but finding the air with which to talk is a struggle. Yet he has seized life. He takes classes in international politics at the University of Washington and savors time with his wife and four grown children.

In both Oregon and Washington, the law is rigorous in determining who is eligible to receive the drugs. Two physicians must confirm that a patient has six months or less to live. And the request for the drugs must be made twice, 15 days apart, before they are handed out. They must be self-administered, which creates a special challenge for people with A.L.S.

Dr. Wesley said he would find a way to meet that requirement, perhaps by tipping a cup into his feeding tube.

The reasons people have given for requesting physician-assisted dying have also defied expectations.

Dr. Linda Ganzini, a professor of psychiatry at Oregon Health and Science University, published a study in 2009 of 56 Oregonians who were in the process of requesting physician-aided dying.

"Everybody thought this was going to be about pain," Dr. Ganzini said. "It turns out pain is kind of irrelevant."

At the time of each of the 56 patients' requests, almost none of them rated pain as a primary motivation. By far the most common reasons, Dr. Ganzini's study found, were the desire to be in control, to remain autonomous and to die at home. "It turns out that for this group of people, dying is less about physical symptoms than personal values," she said.

The proposed law in Massachusetts mirrors those in Oregon and Washington. According to a telephone survey conducted in May by the Polling Institute at Western New England University, 60 percent of the surveyed voters supported "allowing people who are dying to legally obtain medication that they could use to end their lives."

"Support isn't just from progressive Democrats, but conservatives, too," said Stephen Crawford, a spokesman for the Dignity 2012 campaign in Massachusetts, which supports the initiative. "It's even a libertarian issue. The thinking is the government or my doctor won't control my final days."

Such laws have influential opponents, including the Roman Catholic Church, which considers suicide a sin but was an early leader in encouraging terminal patients to consider hospice care. Dr. Christine K. Cassel, a bioethicist who is president of the American Board of

Internal Medicine, credits the church with that effort. "But you can see why they can go right up to that line and not cross over it," she said.

The American Medical Association also opposes physician-assisted dying. Writing prescriptions for the drugs is antithetical to doctors' role as healers, the group says. Many individual physicians share that concern.

"I didn't go into medicine to kill people," said Dr. Kenneth R. Stevens, an emeritus professor of radiation oncology at Oregon Health and Science University and vice president of the Physicians for Compassionate Care Education Foundation.

Dr. Steven Kirtland, who has been Dr. Wesley's pulmonologist for three years, said he had little hesitation about agreeing to Dr. Wesley's request, the only prescription for the drugs that Dr. Kirtland has written.

"I've seen a lot of bad deaths," Dr. Kirtland said. "Part of our job as physicians is to help people have a good death, and, frankly, we need to do more of that."

Dr. Wesley's wife, Virginia Sly, has come to accept her husband's decision. Yet she does not want the pills in the house, and he agrees. "It just feels so negative," she said. So the prescription remains at the pharmacy, with the drugs available within 48 hours.

There are no studies of the psychological effect of having a prescription on hand, but experts say many patients who have received one find comfort in knowing they have or can get the drugs. About a third of those who fill the prescription die without using it. "I don't know if I'll use the medication to end my life," Dr. Wesley said. "But I do know that it is my life, it is my death, and it should be my choice."

A Life-or-Death Situation

BY ROBIN MARANTZ HENIG | JULY 17, 2013

IF MARGARET PABST BATTIN hadn't had a cold that day, she would have joined her husband, Brooke Hopkins, on his bike ride. Instead Peggy (as just about everyone calls her) went to two lectures at the University of Utah, where she teaches philosophy and writes about end-of-life bioethics. Which is why she wasn't with Brooke the moment everything changed.

Brooke was cycling down a hill in City Creek Canyon in Salt Lake City when he collided with an oncoming bicycle around a blind curve, catapulting him onto the mountain path. His helmet cracked just above the left temple, meaning Brooke fell directly on his head, and his body followed in a grotesque somersault that broke his neck at the top of the spine. He stopped breathing, turned purple and might have died if a flight-rescue nurse didn't happen to jog by. The jogger resuscitated and stabilized him, and someone raced to the bottom of the canyon to call 911.

If Peggy had been there and known the extent of Brooke's injury, she might have urged the rescuers not to revive him. Brooke updated a living will the previous year, specifying that should he suffer a grievous illness or injury leading to a terminal condition or vegetative state, he wanted no procedures done that "would serve only to unnaturally prolong the moment of my death and to unnaturally postpone or prolong the dying process." But Peggy wasn't there, and Brooke, who had recently retired as an English professor at the University of Utah, was kept breathing with a hand-pumped air bag during the ambulance ride to University Hospital, three miles away. As soon as he got there, he was attached to a ventilator.

By the time Peggy arrived and saw her husband ensnared in the life-sustaining machinery he hoped to avoid, decisions about intervention already had been made. It was Nov. 14, 2008, late afternoon. She didn't know yet that Brooke would end up a quadriplegic, paralyzed from the shoulders down.

Suffering, suicide, euthanasia, a dignified death — these were subjects she had thought and written about for years, and now, suddenly, they turned unbearably personal. Alongside her physically ravaged husband, she would watch lofty ideas be trumped by reality — and would discover just how messy, raw and muddled the end of life can be.

In the weeks after the accident, Peggy found herself thinking about the title character in Tolstoy's "Death of Ivan Ilyich," who wondered, "What if my whole life has been wrong?" Her whole life had involved writing "wheelbarrows full" of books and articles championing self-determination in dying. And now here was her husband, a plugged-in mannequin in the I.C.U., the very embodiment of a right-to-die case study.

An international leader in bioethics, Peggy explored the right to a good and easeful death by their own hand, if need be, for people who were terminally ill, as well as for those whose lives had become intolerable because of chronic illness, serious injury or extreme old age. She didn't shy away from contentious words like "euthanasia." Nor did she run from fringe groups like NuTech, which is devoted to finding more-efficient methods of what it calls self-deliverance, or Soars (Society for Old Age Rational Suicide), which defends the right of the "very elderly" to choose death as a way to pre-empt old-age catastrophes. She also found common purpose with more-mainstream groups, like Compassion and Choices, that push for legislation or ballot initiatives to allow doctors to help "hasten death" in the terminally ill (which is now permitted, with restrictions, in Oregon, Washington, Montana and Vermont). And she testified in trials on behalf of individuals seeking permission to end their lives legally with the help of a doctor or a loved one.

At the heart of her argument was her belief in autonomy. "The competent patient can, and ought to be accorded the right to, determine what is to be done to him or her, even if ... it means he or she will die," she wrote in 1994 in "The Least Worst Death," the third of her seven books about how we die.

Peggy traces her interest in death to her mother's difficult one, from liver cancer, when Peggy was 21. Only later, when she started to write fiction in an M.F.A. program at the University of California, Irvine, (which she completed while getting her doctorate in philosophy and raising two young children) did she realize how much that event had shaped her thinking. Her short stories "all looked like bioethics problems," she says, wrestling with topics like aging, mental competence, medical research, suicide — moral quandaries she would be mining for the rest of her life.

Fiction allowed her to riff on scenarios more freely than philosophy did, so she sometimes used it in her scholarly writing. In "Ending Life: Ethics and the Way We Die," published in 2005, she included two short stories: a fictional account of an aged couple planning a tandem suicide to make way for the younger generation, until one of them has a change of heart; and a story based on an actual experience in grad school, when Peggy had to help a scientist kill the dogs in his psych experiment. The point of including the second story, she wrote in the book's introduction, was to ground her philosophical arguments in something more elemental, "the unsettling, stomach-disturbing, conscience-trying unease" of being involved in any death, whether through action, as happened in that laboratory, or acquiescence.

When Peggy finished her doctorate in 1976, the right-to-die debate was dominated by the media spectacle around Karen Ann Quinlan, a comatose young woman whose parents went to the New Jersey Supreme Court for permission to withdraw her from life support. It helped Peggy clarify her thoughts about death with dignity and shaped her belief in self-determination as a basic human right. "A person should be accorded the right to live his or her life as they see fit (provided, of course, that this does not significantly harm others), and that includes the very end of their life," she wrote in one of her nearly 40 journal articles on this subject. "That's just the way I see it."

That's the way she saw it after Brooke's accident too, but with a new spiky awareness of what it means to choose death. Scholarly thought experiments were one thing, but this was a man she adored — a man with whom she shared a rich and passionate life for more than 30 years — who was now physically devastated but still free, as she knew he had to be, to make a choice that would cause her anguish.

"It is not just about terminally ill people in general in a kind of abstract way now," she wrote after the accident; "it's also about my husband, Brooke. I still love him, that's a simple fact. What if he wanted to die? Can I imagine standing by while his ventilator was switched off?"

Before the collision, Brooke was known for his gusto. "At parties he was the one who ate the most, drank the most, talked the loudest, danced the longest," one friend recalls. A striking 6-foot-5, he had a winning smile and a mess of steely gray hair and was often off on some adventure with friends. He went on expeditions to the Himalayas, Argentina, Chile, China, Venezuela and more; closer to home, he often cycled, hiked or backcountry skied in the mountains around Salt Lake City. In addition, Brooke, who had a bachelor's degree and a doctorate from Harvard, was a popular English professor who taught British and American literature with a special fondness for the poetry of Wordsworth, Shelley, Byron and Keats.

All that energy went absolutely still at the moment of his collision. When Brooke woke up in the I.C.U., his stepson, Mike, was at the bedside and had to tell Brooke that he might never again walk, turn over or breathe on his own. Brooke remained silent — he was made mute by the ventilation tube down his throat — but he thought of Keats:

The feel of not to feel it,
When there is none to heal it
Nor numbed sense to steel it.

"Those words, 'the feel of not to feel it,' suddenly meant something to me in ways that they never had before," he wrote later on a blog his stepdaughter, Sara, started to keep people apprised of his progress. "My suffering was going to be a drop in the bucket compared to all the human suffering experienced by people throughout human history, but still, it was going to be a suffering nevertheless."

Brooke took some solace in Buddhism, which he began exploring when he was in his 40s. A few weeks after the accident, a local Buddhist teacher, Lama Thupten Dorje Gyaltsen, came to his hospital room. "The body is ephemeral," Lama Thupten declared, gesturing at his own body under his maroon-and-saffron robe. He urged Brooke to focus on his mind. At the time, it was a comfort to think that his mind, which seemed intact, was all that mattered. It meant he could still be the same man he always was even if he never moved again. But as much as he yearned to believe it, Brooke's subsequent experiences — spasms, pain, catheterizations, bouts of pneumonia, infected abscesses in his groin — have made him wary of platitudes. He still wants to believe the mind is everything. But he has learned that no mind can fly free of a useless body's incessant neediness.

One gray morning in February, more than four years after the accident, I met Brooke and Peggy at their home in the Salt Lake City neighborhood known as the Avenues. Brooke rolled into the living room in his motorized wheelchair. It was a month before his 71st birthday, and his handsome face was animated by intense, shiny brown eyes, deep-set under a bristly awning of brow. He was dressed as usual: a pullover, polyester pants that snap open all the way down each leg, a diaper and green Crocs. A friend was reading on a couch nearby, a caregiver was doing her schoolwork in the kitchen and Peggy had retreated upstairs to her office amid towers of papers, books and magazines. She had finally gained some momentum on a project that was slowed by Brooke's accident: a compendium of philosophical writings about suicide, dating as far back as Aristotle.

Peggy, who is 72, still works full time. This lets her hold on to the university's excellent health insurance, which covers a large portion of Brooke's inpatient care and doctor bills, with Medicare paying most of the rest of them. But even with this double coverage, Peggy spends a lot of time arguing with insurance companies that balk at expenditures like his $45,000 wheelchair. And she still pays a huge amount of the cost, including nearly $250,000 a year to Brooke's caregivers, 12 mostly young and devoted health care workers who come in shifts so there's always at least one on duty. Peggy says she and Brooke were lucky to have had a healthy retirement fund at the time of the accident, but she doesn't know how many more years they will be able to sustain this level of high-quality 24-hour care.

Scattered around the living room were counter-height stools that Peggy picked up at yard sales. She urges visitors to pull them up to Brooke's wheelchair, because he's tall and the stools bring most people to eye level. About two years ago, Brooke used a ventilator only when he slept, but following a series of infections and other setbacks, he was now on the ventilator many of his waking hours, too, along with a diaphragmatic pacer that kept his breathing regular. Earlier that morning his caregiver adjusted the ventilator so he and I could talk, deflating the cuff around his tracheostomy tube to allow air to pass over his larynx. This let him speak the way everyone does, vocalizing as he exhaled. It seemed to tire him, though; his pauses became longer as our conversation went on. But whenever I suggested that we stop for a while so he could rest, Brooke insisted that he wanted to keep talking.

What he wanted to talk about was how depressed he was. He recognized the feeling, having struggled with bipolar disorder since adolescence. "It takes a long time to get ready for anything," he said about his life now. "To get up in the morning, which I kind of hate, to have every day be more or less the same as every other day . . . and then to spend so much time going to bed. Day after day, day after day, day after day."

Brooke has good days and bad days. When friends are around playing blues harmonica or reading aloud to him, when his mind is clear and his body is not in pain — that's a good day. On a good day, he said, he feels even more creative than he was in his able-bodied life, and his relationships with Peggy, his two stepchildren and his many friends are richer and more intimate than before; he has no time or patience for small talk, and neither do they. Every so often he'll turn to Peggy and announce, "I love my life."

On a good day, Brooke's voice is strong, which lets him keep up with reading and writing with voice-recognition software. A caregiver arranges a Bluetooth microphone on his head, and he dictates e-mail and races through books by calling out, "Page down," when he reaches the bottom of a screen. On a good day, he also might get outside for a while. "I like to take long walks, quote unquote, in the park," he told me. "There's a graveyard somewhat lugubriously next to us that I like to go through," pushed in his wheelchair by a caregiver with Peggy alongside. A couple of years ago, he and Peggy bought two plots there; they get a kick out of visiting their burial sites and taking in the view.

But on bad days these pleasures fade, and everything about his current life seems bleak. These are days when physical problems — latent infections, low oxygen levels, drug interactions or, in a cruel paradox of paralysis, severe pain in his motionless limbs — can lead to exhaustion, depression, confusion and even hallucinations. As Brooke described these darker times, Peggy came down from her office and sat nearby, half-listening. She has bright blue eyes and a pretty, freckled face fringed by blond-white hair. Most days she wears jeans and running shoes and a slightly distracted expression. She takes long hikes almost daily, and once a week tries to squeeze in a Pilates session to help treat her scoliosis. Each body harbors its own form of decay, and this is Peggy's; the scoliosis is getting worse as she ages.

She walked over to us, bent crookedly at the waist, and gently kissed Brooke's forehead. "Depression is not uncommon in winter," she said in the soft voice she almost always uses with him. "It's important to think positive thoughts."

"Basically I dislike being dependent, that's all," he said, looking hard into her eyes. He spit some excess saliva into a cup.

"It's something you never complain about," she said. "You're not a big complainer."

"One thing I don't like is people speaking for me, though."

Peggy looked a bit stung. "And that includes me?" she asked.

"Yes," he said, still looking into her eyes. "I don't like that."

She made an effort not to get defensive. "Well, sometimes that has to happen, for me to speak for you," she began. "But . . . but not always. I try not to."

Brooke seemed sorry to have spoken up; it was clear he didn't want to hurt her. "I'm trying to be as frank as possible," he said.

"No, it's good," she assured him, her protective instincts clicking in. "It helps me for you to say that, to tell me what you would have wanted to say instead."

All Brooke could muster was a raspy, "Yep."

"The most important thing is to not speak for someone else," Peggy insisted.

"Yep," Brooke repeated. "What I want to do most right now is be quiet and read." So Peggy and I left him in the living room, where the big-screen monitor was queued up to Chapter 46 of "Moby-Dick." "Page down," he called out, forced to keep repeating it like a mantra because his speech was croaky and the software had trouble recognizing the phrase. "Page down. Page down."

For Brooke, what elevates his life beyond the day-to-day slog of maintaining it — the vast team effort required to keep his inert sack of a body fed and dressed and clean and functioning — is his continuing ability to teach part time through the University of Utah's adult-education program. During my February visit, I sat in on one of his classes, which he teaches with Michael Rudick, another retired English professor from the university. Some two dozen students, most over 60, crammed into Brooke's living room for a discussion of "Moby-Dick." Conversation turned to the mind-body problem. "Melville is making fun here of Descartes, as though you could exist as a mind without a body," said Howard Horwitz, who teaches in the English department and was helping out that day.

Brooke seemed exhausted and sat quietly, impassive as Buddha as his ventilator sighed. At one point a student called out to ask what

Brooke thought about a particular passage. He responded with an oblique, "I'd much rather hear what you think," and was silent for the rest of the class. The discussion continued with the two other professors taking charge. There was an almost forced animation, as if the students had tacitly agreed to cover for a man they loved, admired and were worried about.

When Peggy arrived late — she was at a meeting on campus — Brooke flashed her one of his dazzling smiles. His eyes stayed on her as she positioned herself near an old baby grand that hugs a corner of the living room, a memento from Brooke's parents' house in Baltimore. Above the piano is a huge painting that Peggy got years ago, a serial self-portrait of a dark-haired figure with a mustache — six full-body images of the same man in various stages of disappearing.

"He's never looked this bad," Peggy whispered to me during the break as students milled around. She went to Brooke and kissed his forehead. "Are you O.K.?" she asked softly.

"I'm fine," he said. "Don't worry."

They have this exchange a lot: Peggy leaning in to ask if he's O.K., Brooke telling her not to worry, Peggy worrying anyway. Quietly, so the students wouldn't hear, she asked the respiratory therapist on duty, Jaycee Carter, when Brooke last had his CoughAssist therapy, a method that forces out mucus that can clog his lungs. "Three hours ago," Jaycee said. But Brooke said he didn't want it while the class was there: it's noisy, and it brings up a lot of unsightly phlegm. As students started to head back to their seats, Peggy lit on a more discreet alternative: a spritz of albuterol, used in asthma inhalers to relax the airways, into his trach tube. Jaycee stood by awaiting instructions, Brooke kept shaking his head — no albuterol, not now, no — and Peggy kept insisting. At last, annoyance prickling his expressive eyebrows, he gave in, and Jaycee did as she was told. But the albuterol didn't help.

Peggy retreated to the piano as the class resumed, her eyes brimming. "This is bad," she murmured. "This is really bad." Underlying her anxiety was a frightening possibility: that Brooke's inability to teach that day was the start of a progressive decline. Up until then, his occasional mental fogginess was always explained by something transient, like an infection. But if he were to lose his intellectual functioning, he would be robbed of all the things that still give his life meaning: teaching, writing and interacting with the people he loves. If that day ever came, it would provoke a grim reckoning, forcing Brooke to rethink — provided he was still capable of thinking — whether this is a life worth holding onto.

After class, Jaycee wheeled Brooke to the dining area so he could sit with Peggy and me as we ate dinner. Brooke doesn't eat anymore. Last August he had a feeding tube inserted as a way to avoid the dangerous infections and inflammations that were constantly sending him to the hospital. If he doesn't chew, drink or swallow, there's less chance that food or fluid will end up in his lungs and cause aspiration pneumonia.

In his prior life, Brooke couldn't have imagined tolerating a feeding tube; he loved eating too much. In fact, when he updated his living will in 2007, he specifically noted his wish to avoid "administration of sustenance and hydration." But the document had a caveat found in most advance directives, one that has proved critical in negotiating his care since the accident: "I reserve the right to give current medical directions to physicians and other providers of medical services so long as I am able," even if they conflict with the living will.

Thus a man who had always taken great joy in preparing, sharing and savoring food decided to give up his final sensory pleasure in order to go on living. He swears he doesn't miss it. He had already been limited to soft, easy-to-swallow foods with no seeds or crunchiness — runny eggs, yogurt, mashed avocado. And as much as he loved the social aspects of eating, the long conversations over the last of the wine, he managed, with some gentle prodding from Peggy, to think of the feeding tube as a kind of liberation. After all, as she explained on the family blog, Brooke could still do "almost all the important things that are part of the enjoyment of food" — he could still smell its aroma, admire its presentation, join in on the mealtime chatter, even sample a morsel the way a wine taster might, chewing it and then discreetly spitting it out. Maybe, she wrote, "being liberated from the crass bodily necessity of eating brings you a step closer to some sort of nirvana."

Or as Brooke put it to me in his unvarnished way: "You can get used to anything."

Brooke kept nodding off as he sat watching us eat — the class had really drained him — but Peggy kept him up until 9 o'clock, when his hourlong bedtime ritual begins. After Jaycee brought him to his room, she and the night-shift caregiver hoisted him from his wheelchair and into the bed using an elaborate system of ceiling tracks, slings and motorized lifts; changed him into a hospital gown; washed his face and brushed his teeth; emptied his bladder with a catheter; strapped on booties and finger splints to position his extremities; hooked him up to the ventilator; and set up four cans of Replete Fiber to slowly drip into his feeding tube as he slept. The ritual ended with what Brooke and Peggy think of as the most important part of the day, when Brooke finally is settled into bed and Peggy takes off her shoes and climbs in, too, keeping him company until he gets sleepy. (Peggy sleeps in a new bedroom she had built upstairs.) There they lie, side by side in his double-wide hospital bed, their heads close on the pillow, talking in the low, private rumbles of any intimate marriage.

Throughout the first half of last year, Brooke had severe pain in his back and legs, and all the remedies he tried — acupuncture, cortisone shots, pressure-point therapy, nerve-impulse scrambling — were useless. At one point last summer, he decided he couldn't go on living that way. "Pain eats away at your soul," he wrote on July 28, 2012, using his voice-recognition software to dictate what he called a "Final Letter" to his loved ones, explaining why he now wanted to die:

> *For many years since the accident I have been motivated by a deep will to live and to contribute to the benefit of others in my small way. I think I have done that. And I am proud of it. But as I have told Peggy over the past few months, I knew that I would reach a limit to what I could do. And I have arrived at the limit over the past couple of weeks.*

He had thoughts like this before, but this time it felt different to Peggy, who proofread and typed the letter; the longing for death felt like something carefully considered, something serious and sincere. This was an autonomous, fully alert person making a decision about his own final days — the very situation she had spent her career defending. She reasoned that Brooke had the right, as a mentally competent patient, to reject medical interventions that could further prolong his life, even though he did not live in a state where assisted suicide was explicitly legal. And if he wanted to reject those interventions now, after four years of consenting to every treatment, Peggy was ready to help. She shifted from being Brooke's devoted lifeline to being the midwife to his death.

She knew from a hospice nurse that one way to ease a patient's dying included morphine for "air hunger," Haldol for "delusions and end-of-life agitation" and Tylenol suppositories for "end-of-life fever, 99 to 101 degrees." Another nurse mentioned morphine, Haldol and the sedative Ativan; a third talked about Duragesic patches to deliver fentanyl, a potent opium alternative used for pain. Peggy also tried to find out whether cardiologists would ever be willing to order deactivation of a pacemaker at a very ill patient's request (probably, she was told). She kept pages of scribbled notes in a blue folder marked "Death and Dying." She had also taken careful notes when Brooke started to talk about his funeral. He told her what music he wanted, including a few gospel songs by Marion Williams, and which readings from Wordsworth's "Lucy Poems" and Whitman's "Leaves of Grass." On his gravestone, he might like a line from Henry Adams: "A teacher affects eternity; he can never tell where his influence stops." These were good conversations, but they left him, he told Peggy, "completely emotionally torn up."

Then in early August, fluid started accumulating in Brooke's chest cavity, a condition known as pleural effusion, and he had trouble breathing, even on the ventilator. He was uncomfortable and becoming delirious. Other people, including a few of Brooke's caregivers, might have seen this as a kind of divine intervention — a rapid deterioration just when Brooke was longing for death anyway, easing him into a final release. But that's not how Peggy saw it. This was not the death Brooke wanted, confused and in pain, she explained to me later; he had always spoken of a "generous death" for which he was alert, calm, present and surrounded by people he loved. So she consulted with a physician at the hospital about whether Brooke would improve if doctors there extracted the fluid that was causing the respiratory distress. In the end, she decided to ignore the "Final Letter." She went upstairs, got dressed and, along with the caregiver on duty, put Brooke into the wheelchair-accessible van in the driveway and drove him to the emergency room.

This put Brooke back in the hospital with heavy-duty antibiotics treating yet another lung problem. During his three-week stay he recovered enough to make his own medical decisions again — which is when he consented to the insertion of the feeding tube. He also met with a palliative-care expert, who suggested trying one more pain treatment: low-dose methadone around the clock, five milligrams at exactly 9 a.m. and exactly 9 p.m., every day. With the methadone, Brooke's pain was at last manageable. Now when he reflects on that hospitalization, he thinks of it as having a "happy ending." In the "Death and Dying" folder is one last penciled note from Peggy dated Aug. 18, 2012: "10:37 a.m. Brooke says he wants to 'soldier on' despite difficulties."

A couple of days after Brooke and Peggy talked about his not wanting anyone to speak for him, the subject came up again. Peggy raised it as we all sat in the living room. At first she did all the talking, unwittingly acting out the very problem under discussion. So I interrupted with a direct question to Brooke. Why, I asked, do you think Peggy sometimes does the talking for you?

"I think it's because she's concerned about me and wants the best for me," he said. He made the gesture I'd watched him make before, lifting the tops of his shoulders, over which he still has motor control, in a resigned-looking little shrug. In light of such pervasive dependency, that shrug seemed to say, how can a loving, well-meaning wife help but sometimes overstep in her eagerness to anticipate her husband's needs?

I asked Brooke if Peggy ever misunderstood what he meant to say.

"I don't know, ask her," he said. But Peggy saw the irony there and urged Brooke to speak up for himself.

"Occasionally, yes," he said, though he couldn't think of any specific instances.

When she makes a mistake, I asked, do you ever correct her?

"No, because I don't want to upset her." His brown eyes got very big.

She: "It would be O.K."

He: "O.K."

She: "It would help me if you would say to me — "

He: "O.K., O.K., O.K."

She: "I think this issue is especially important. . . . What you've wanted has fluctuated a lot, and part of it is to try to figure out what's genuine and what's a part of response to the pain. That's the hardest part for me, when you say: 'I don't want to go to the hospital ever again, I don't like being in the hospital and I don't want to be sick. If the choice is going to the hospital or dying, I'll take the dying.' "

Peggy turned to me. She wanted me to understand her thinking on this. It's so hard to know what Brooke wants, she explained, because there have been times when she has taken him to the hospital, and he later says that she made the right call. It's so hard, she repeated. She has to be able to hear how a transient despair differs from a deep and abiding decision to die. She believes he hasn't made that deep, abiding decision yet, despite the "Final Letter."

She understands him well enough, she told me, to know when his apparent urgency is just a reflection of his dramatic way of presenting things: his deep voice, his massive size, his grimaces. "Brooke is very expressive when he's in his full self," she said.

Watching the dependence, indignity and sheer physical travail that

Brooke must live through every day, Peggy told me, she doesn't think she would have the stamina to endure a devastating injury like his. "It seems not what I'd want," she said when I asked if she would choose to stay alive if she were paralyzed. While she might not want to persevere in such a constrained and difficult life, she believes that Brooke does want to, and she tends to interpret even his most anguished cries in a way that lets her conclude that he doesn't quite mean what he says. But she worries that others in his life, even the caregivers who have become so close to him, might not be able to calibrate the sincerity of those over-the-top pleas and might leap too quickly to follow his instructions if he yelled out about wanting to end it all.

Suzy Quirantes, the senior member of the caregiving team, a trained respiratory therapist who has been with Brooke since the day he came home in 2010, sees it a bit differently. "I've worked with death a lot," she told me. She thinks there have been times when Peggy has been unable to hear Brooke's heartfelt expressions of a desire to die. "Last year, right after the feeding tube, he kept refusing his therapies," she said. "And I said, 'If you're really serious, if you're done, I need you to be very clear, and you need to be able to talk to Peggy so she understands.'" He never did talk to Peggy, though — maybe because he wasn't clear in his own mind what he wanted. "He has said, 'I'm done,' and then when we kind of talk more about it, he gets scared," Suzy said. "He says: 'What I mean is I'm done doing this stuff in the hospital. But I'm not ready to die yet.'"

The tangled, sometimes contradictory nature of Brooke's feelings has led to subtle shifts in Peggy's scholarly thinking. She still believes that, whenever possible, people have the right to choose when and how to die. But she now better understands how vast and terrifying that choice really is. "What has changed," she told me, "is my sense of how extremely complex, how extremely textured, any particular case is." This realization is infinitely more fraught when you're inextricably invested in the outcome and when the signals your loved one sends are not only hard to read but also are constantly in flux.

The only consistent choice Brooke has made — and he's made it again and again every time he gives informed consent for a feeding tube or a diaphragmatic pacer, every time he permits treatment of an infection or a bedsore — is the one to stay alive. This is the often-unspoken flip side of the death-with-dignity movement that Peggy has long been a part of. Proponents generally focus on only one branch of the decision tree: the moment of choosing death. There's much talk of living wills, D.N.R. orders, suicide, withdrawal of life support, exit strategies. Brooke's experience has forced Peggy to step back from that moment to an earlier one: the moment of confronting one's own horrific circumstances and choosing, at least for now, to keep on living. But the reasons for that choice are complicated too. Brooke told me that he knows Peggy is a strong person who will recover from his death and move on. But he has also expressed a desire not to abandon her. And Peggy worries that sometimes Brooke is saying he wants to keep fighting and stay alive not because that's what he wants, but because he thinks that's what she wants him to want. And to further complicate things, it's not even clear what Peggy really wants him to want. Her own desires seem to shift from day to day. One thing that doesn't change, though: She is deeply afraid of misunderstanding Brooke's wishes in a way that can't be undone. The worst outcome, to her, would be to think that this time he really does want to die and then to feel as if she might have been wrong.

Since Brooke's accident, Peggy has continued to advocate for people seeking to die. She went to Vancouver in late 2011 to testify in court in the case of Gloria Taylor, a woman with ALS who wanted help ending her life when she was ready. And in 2012, she presented testimony by Skype in the case of Marie Fleming, an Irishwoman with multiple sclerosis who was making a similar request. The plaintiffs were a lot like Brooke, cognitively intact with progressively more useless bodies. But they felt a need to go to court to assure they would have control in the timing of their own deaths. Brooke has not. Perhaps that's because he believes that Peggy will follow through on a plan to help him die if that's what he ultimately chooses.

Those seeking to end their lives are up against opponents who say that helping the terminally ill to die will lead eventually to pressure being put on vulnerable people — the elderly, the poor, the chronically disabled, the mentally ill — to agree to die to ease the burden on the rest of us. Peggy doesn't buy it. The scholarly work she is most proud of is a study she conducted in 2007, which is one of the first to look empirically at whether people are being coerced into choosing to end their lives. Peggy was reassured when she and her colleagues found that in Oregon and the Netherlands, two places that allow assisted dying, the people who used it tended to be better off and more educated than the people in groups considered vulnerable.

What Peggy has become more aware of now is the possibility of the opposite, more subtle, kind of coercion — not the influence of a greedy relative or a cost-conscious state that wants you to die, but pressure from a much-loved spouse or partner who wants you to live. The very presence of these loved ones undercuts the notion of true autonomy. We are social beings, and only the unluckiest of us live in a vacuum; for most, there are always at least a few people who count on us, adore us and have a stake in what we decide. Everyone's autonomy abuts someone else's.

During Peggy's cross-examination in the Gloria Taylor trial, the Canadian government's lawyer tried to argue that Brooke's choice to keep living weakened Peggy's argument in favor of assisted suicide. Isn't it true, the lawyer asked, that "this accident presented some pretty profoundly serious challenges to your thinking on the subject?"

Yes, Peggy said, but only by provoking the "concerted re-re-rethinking" that any self-respecting philosopher engages in. She remained committed to two moral constructs in end-of-life decision making: autonomy and mercy. "Only where both are operating — that is, where the patient wants to die and dying is the only acceptable way for the patient to avoid pain and suffering — is there a basis for physician-assisted dying," she told the court in an affidavit. "Neither principle is sufficient in and of itself and, in tandem, the two principles operate as safeguards against abuse."

One morning in April, I called to speak with Peggy and Brooke. Peggy told me that when I was there in February, Brooke had an undiagnosed urinary tract infection that affected both his body and his clarity of thinking. It had since cleared up, she said. "He's a different person than the one you saw." The possibility that he'd begun a true cognitive decline was averted, at least for the time being.

"I'm cautiously happy about life in general," Brooke said on speakerphone, stopping between phrases to catch his breath. "I'm getting stronger. Working hard. Loving my teaching. My friends and caregivers. My wife."

I asked about Brooke's "Final Letter" from last summer. I was still trying to understand why Peggy had ignored it, just days after she typed it up for him, and instead took him to the E.R. to treat his pleural effusion. Why hadn't she just let the infection end his life?

"Brooke had always said, 'I'm willing to go to the hospital for something that's reversible, but I don't want to die in the hospital,' " she said, as Brooke listened in on the speakerphone. So she had to "intuit" whether this was something reversible, and she believed it was. "This didn't feel like the end," she said, "but of course you don't know that for sure." In addition, there was that image in her mind of Brooke's ideal of a "generous death." It's hard to say whether she'll ever think conditions are exactly right for the kind of death Brooke wants.

The next day I learned that a few hours after my phone call, Brooke suddenly became agitated and started to yell. "Something bad is happening," he boomed. "I'm not going to make it through the morning." Peggy and the caregiver on duty, Jaycee, tried to figure out what might have brought this on, just hours after he told me he was "cautiously happy." He had gone the previous two nights without his usual Klonopin, which treats his anxiety; maybe that was the explanation. Or maybe discussing his "Final Letter" with me, remembering the desperation of that time, had upset him. He was also getting ready for the first class of a new semester, covering the second half of

"Moby-Dick"; maybe he was experiencing the same teaching anxiety that had plagued him his whole career.

Deciding that Brooke was having a panic attack, Peggy told Jaycee to give him half a dose of Klonopin. She did, but things got worse. Brooke's eyes flashed with fear, and he yelled to Peggy that he was about to do something terrible to her — meaning, she guessed, that he was going to die and leave her alone. Finally he announced that he wanted to turn off all the machines. Everything. He wanted to be disconnected from all the tubes and hoses that were keeping him alive. He was ready to die.

Peggy and Jaycee did what he asked. They turned off the ventilator and disconnected it from the trach, and placed a cap at the opening in his throat. They turned off the oxygen. They turned off the external battery for the diaphragmatic pacer. They showed Brooke that everything was disconnected.

Brooke sat back in his wheelchair then and closed his eyes. There were no tears, no formal goodbyes; it all happened too quickly for that. He sat there waiting to die, ready to die, and felt an incredible sense of calm.

Two minutes passed. Three minutes passed. He opened his eyes and saw Peggy and Jaycee sitting on stools, one on either side, watching him.

"Is this a dream?" he asked.

"No, it's not a dream."

"I didn't die?"

To Brooke, it was a kind of miracle — all the machinery had been shut off, just as he asked, but he was still alive. He felt refreshed, as if he had made it through some sort of trial. He asked Jaycee to reattach everything, and three hours later, after he had a nap, his students arrived to start the new semester, and Brooke began teaching "Moby-Dick" again.

But it was no miracle. "I know what his medical condition is," Peggy told me later, out of Brooke's earshot. "The reason he didn't die is he's not at the moment fully vent-dependent anymore. He can go without oxygen for a while, and he can go with the pacer turned off for some time." She didn't say any of this to Brooke. "It seems to have been such an epiphany, such a discovery, when he woke up and discovered he was still alive," she said. "I don't really want to puncture that bubble."

If for some reason Brooke had become unconscious, she and Jaycee would have revived him, Peggy told me, because she didn't believe he really wanted to die. She thinks what he really wanted was to believe he had a measure of control, that he could ask for an end to his life and be heard. "We showed him that we would do what he asked for," she said, "and he thought it was real." But it wasn't real, I said. It all sounded like an elaborate end-of-life placebo, an indication that in fact he was not in control, that he wasn't being heard. Peggy laughed and did not disagree.

She's not good at keeping secrets from Brooke, though, and by the time I contacted them both by Skype later in the week, she'd told him the truth about that afternoon. In retrospect, Brooke said, the whole thing seemed kind of comical. He mimed it for me, leaning back with his eyes closed waiting for the end to come, then slowly opening them, raising his eyebrows practically to his hairline, overacting like a silent-film star tied to the tracks who slowly realizes the distant train will never arrive. He looked good, handsome in his burgundy polo shirt, mugging for the webcam. Some new crisis, some new decision, was inevitable — in fact, last month it took the form of another farewell letter, stating his desire to die in the spring of 2014, which is when he expects to be finished teaching his next course, on "Don Quixote." But at that moment, Brooke was feeling good. "I think it will be a productive summer," he said. And he and Peggy smiled.

ROBIN MARANTZ HENIG is a contributing writer for the magazine and co-author, with her daughter Samantha Henig, of "Twentysomething: Why Do Young Adults Seem Stuck?"

Brittany Maynard, 'Death With Dignity' Ally, Dies at 29

BY DANIEL E. SLOTNIK | NOV. 3, 2014

BRITTANY MAYNARD, who became a public face for the "death with dignity" movement in the United States after she was found to have terminal brain cancer, ended her life on Saturday at her home in Portland, Ore. She was 29.

Her death, from barbiturates, was confirmed by her husband, Daniel Diaz, who noted that in accordance with Oregon law her death certificate listed a brain tumor as the cause.

Ms. Maynard learned she had brain cancer on New Year's Day this year. Her doctors told her at first that she could live for several years, but after further tests they revised the prognosis in April, saying she had only about six months.

"After months of research, my family and I reached a heartbreaking conclusion: There is no treatment that would save my life, and the recommended treatments would have destroyed the time I had left," Ms. Maynard wrote in a post on CNN's website.

Ms. Maynard decided that when her condition became unbearable she would end her life with medication. She had to uproot her family from her home in Alamo, Calif., and move to Oregon to receive the barbiturates legally.

"Brittany's take on this issue was that it just seems ridiculous that we couldn't live out her final months comfortably in our own home," Mr. Diaz said in an interview on Monday.

Ms. Maynard contacted Compassion & Choices, an end-of-life rights advocacy group, which helped promote a video she posted on YouTube in early October and a second released a few days ago. The videos have been viewed more than 13 million times, and she was interviewed for an article by People magazine. Her story drew international news coverage.

So-called "death with dignity" laws have been passed in five states but are opposed by many political and religious organizations. Many people publicly asked Ms. Maynard to reconsider her decision, including one woman also dying of cancer.

Ms. Maynard defended her right to decide.

"I would not tell anyone else that he or she should choose death with dignity," she wrote on the CNN website. "My question is: Who has the right to tell me that I don't deserve this choice?"

Brittany Lauren Maynard was born on Nov. 19, 1984, in Anaheim, Calif. She received a bachelor's degree in psychology from the University of California, Berkeley, in 2006 and a master's in education from the University of California, Irvine, in 2010.

She married Mr. Diaz in Sonoma, Calif., in 2012 and taught school in Danville, Calif. An ardent traveler, she had explored Southeast Asia and parts of Central and South America.

Besides her husband, she is survived by her mother, Deborah Ziegler, and her stepfather, Gary Holmes.

Ms. Maynard continued traveling during her last months, visiting Alaska, Yellowstone National Park and the Grand Canyon. Being able to choose when to die, she said, allowed her to live.

"It has given me a sense of peace during a tumultuous time that otherwise would be dominated by fear, uncertainty and pain," she wrote.

Casualties of War

OPINION | BY ANN M. ALTMAN | NOV. 7, 2015

IT HAS BEEN 15 YEARS since my mother called and asked, "Do you have some time at the end of July or the beginning of August? Your father and I have decided to kill ourselves and we would like you to come and find our bodies."

My parents, who lived in England, were Czech refugees from the Holocaust. My father, a 26-year-old newly minted lawyer, escaped deportation in 1939 by walking across the border from his native Czechoslovakia into Poland, with England as his goal. My mother's parents put her on a train in Prague, with Shanghai as her eventual destination. She was 18.

My mother's parents died in Lodz and Auschwitz. My father told me that his father had committed suicide during the transport of Jews from Ostrava to Nisko in 1939. This information might have come from his mother, who was deported to Minsk and murdered there in 1942.

During the early years of World War II, chance and good fortune brought both my parents to London, where they met and married in 1945. Within a couple of years, they had established themselves as an academic couple with two children and started to make their way up the social and economic ladder. Their careers were distinguished, with honors and privileges bestowed by their adopted country.

They had made it clear for as long as I can remember that, because of the deaths of all four of their parents in the Holocaust, their lives were their own, to continue or end as they saw fit and whenever they saw fit. They had even made a pact wherein, if one of them died, the other need stay alive for only six months before taking his or her own life, if that life proved unbearable.

My mother's health began to fail in 2000 and, with her phone call from England, it was clear that my parents had abandoned their pact and were planning to end their lives together.

In answer to my mother's macabre question, I said, "I can come to England on the night that you kill yourselves and then come to the house with a doctor and the police, if that is what you want." But, no, that was not what my mother wanted.

"We would like you to come and say goodbye to us, to go to London for the day, and then to return alone to find our bodies." I'm not that tough; I could not agree to do that. So my mother said that they would make other arrangements.

A few weeks later, in mid-August, a doctor was called to their house and found my parents dead, with garbage bags tied over their heads and pillows resting on their suffocated faces. She also found a statement of their intent to kill themselves.

In October, the coroner ruled, "I have to be sure beyond reasonable doubt that both these persons intended to take their own lives. They have done so, I am sure."

We shall all die and most of us want some control over the manner of our dying. Some want to be sure that they will be able to kill themselves; some want the right to assisted suicide if they are unable to kill themselves; some want purely palliative care; and some want every possible medical intervention.

I hope, too, to have some control over my dying and I am repelled neither by the idea of suicide nor by the idea of assisted suicide. However, my experience with my parents' deaths gives me pause.

Since my parents' deaths, many of my friends have seen their parents die in the hospital or under hospice care. I envy all these friends. Their parents brought them into this world and they were there for their parents when their parents left this world. By depriving me of this filial role, my parents rejected me more forcefully than they could possibly have understood — or, maybe, they just did not care. Or was their request that I be the one to find their bodies an indication of their great love for me? This is a question that I can never answer.

Most of the time, I do not think of my parents' deaths. But they are a result of the Holocaust as surely as the deaths of my grandparents.

And it is at the most inopportune times, when I am worried about my own health, that I have to confront all six deaths. When a physician asks for my family history, I have to say, "My grandparents perished as Jews in the Holocaust; my father died, according to his autopsy, in perfect health; and my parents killed themselves."

Sherwin Nuland, the author of "How We Die," taught me that one cannot control how one dies but one can have some control over how one lives. But I wonder how much control I shall have over my own death and, more profoundly, how much control is best for me and, even more important, for my children and grandchildren. It is my descendants, after all, who will be dealing with the manner and consequences of my death when I am gone.

ANN M. ALTMAN is a scientist, a writer and a political adviser.

The Last Thing Mom Asked

OPINION | BY SARAH LYALL | AUG. 31, 2018

I am not a doctor. I am not very brave. But I want to do what she wants.

I AM ABOUT to kill my mother.

I am looking for a way to put this off as long as possible, and so I start watching one of the final episodes of the TV drama "The Americans." Today, Keri Russell, playing a Russian agent, is spying on a State Department official by posing as a nurse for his terminally ill wife.

The agent is a stone-cold murderer, but she feels desperately sorry for the official, whose attempts to help his wife kill herself with morphine have left her in a gasping, not-dead limbo. So Keri Russell finishes the job by shoving a paintbrush down the woman's throat and holding a plastic bag over her head.

This is not a good time to be watching this particular scene.

Right now my mother is in bed across the hall, in the endgame of Stage 4 lung cancer. She is nearly 83, she has had enough, and she is ready to die. More specifically, she is ready to have me help her die.

I can see her point.

An unsentimental, practical person, she has for many years been preparing for the moment when death would become more alluring than life. We have talked about it nonstop since she received her diagnosis about three months ago and, like Gloria Swanson going up in a blaze of grand pronouncements, declared that she intended to forgo chemotherapy.

"I would rather die than lose my hair," she said airily to the startled oncologist, before terrorizing the hospital physiotherapist by snapping: "I could be dead in three months. Do you really think it's going to make a difference if I get out of bed and walk around for five minutes now?"

So she went home to die. She was her regular funny, astringent self.

"Just put a pillow over my head," she would say, only half joking, when I saw her each evening. "Am I dead yet?" she'd say in the morning, genuinely annoyed that terminal cancer was refusing to adhere to her imagined timetable.

Gradually, the illness took hold, the inevitable became less abstract and the jokes stopped. Mom had vivid dreams of death so awful that she could not bring herself to describe them. She became too weak to leave her bed, more of her independence seeping out each day like air from a balloon. Her world closed in.

Lung cancer is a frightening illness. In its final stages, it can make you feel as though you're drowning, or suffocating. A formidable pharmacological stew of medications can help to suppress the symptoms, but no pill can take away the pain of waking up each day and remembering all over again that you are about to die.

I know what I'm supposed to do, because she has told me many times. One of the stories passed down as gospel in our tiny family is about how my late father, a doctor, helped his own mother — my grand-mother Cecilia, whom I never met — at the end of her life. Her cancer was unbearable. "So he gave her a big dose of morphine to stop the pain," my mother has always told my brother and me, as if reaching the end of a fairy tale. "It had the side effect of stopping her heart."

As it happens, I have a big dose of morphine right here in the house. I also have some hefty doses of codeine, Ambien, Haldol and Ativan that I've cunningly stockpiled from the hospice service, like a squirrel hoarding for winter. In my top drawer, next to Mom's passport, are more than 100 micrograms worth of fentanyl patches — enough to kill her and several passers-by.

But I am not a trained assassin. I am not a doctor. I am not very brave. I'm just a person who wants to do the most important thing that her mother has ever asked of her. I'm also a resident of New York State, where assisted suicide is illegal.

Mom has taken to drifting off in the middle of crucial sentences. "It's important to remember the. ..." she announces. "The one thing I need to tell you is. ..." But in coherent moments she looks at me with a clarity that shreds my heart. My strong mother. "Oh, Sarah," she says. "I'm in so much pain."

So it's time. I begin counting up the drugs. But then I watch the bungled assisted suicide scene in "The Americans" and I see how easy it is to get wrong and I get scared. Often patients develop a tolerance for morphine, Keri Russell is saying in her guise as hospice nurse, explaining why the higher dose did not kill the dying wife.

How much is the right amount, I wonder, a morphine bottle in my hand. What if Mom chokes, vomits, falls into a half-dead limbo, wakes up and yells at me? How are you supposed to do this? I have no prob-lem with the idea of committing murder on behalf of a dying person you love, but I can't ask anyone else — the health aides, my brother — for help, since I don't want to implicate them in my crime.

Panicked, I go online and start calling end-of-life organizations. The people are endlessly compassionate, but no one will, or can, tell me what dosage to give, or how to give it. I try to talk to one of the hospice workers, but she threatens to report me to the police. "We are not having this conversation," she says.

Oh, yes, we are. She tries another tack. "If you do this, you'll never forgive yourself," she says. Actually, I tell her, I'll never forgive myself if I don't.

But I can't do it. I can't do it. I promised, but I can't.

Families are complicated and mother-daughter relationships are perhaps the most complicated of all. I've had a lifetime of feeling unable to get anything right, really, with my mother.

"Mom," I say finally. I don't want to bring this up. It's so late, and she's so weak and she's drifting in and out and why didn't we consider this particular eventuality before, the one where I lose my nerve. But. One thing you can do, I tell her, is to stop eating and drinking. We'll make you comfortable. We'll give you so many drugs that you won't even know. It'll be like sleeping.

About 20 minutes later, she emerges from her drugged state. "I'm ready," she says clearly, "to fall asleep and not wake up."

The next day she wakes up. This is how incompetent I am. "You swore this wouldn't happen, Sarah," she says, her voice vibrating with fury. "I'm so sorry, Mama," I say, crying as I drip more narcotics into her mouth with a syringe.

She lies in twilight for the next few days. But sometimes her eyes open in a panic and dart around, full of fear. It feels as if everything has become very primal, requiring an instinct for improvisation I don't have.

So I do what has always soothed me, ever since I was old enough to read. I pick up "Charlotte's Web" and read the last two chapters — aloud, this time — the ones where Charlotte dies after living her singular, stylish life, and three of her chatty spider babies build little webs in the corner of the barn so they can stay with Wilbur the pig.

I always cried when I read this part to my daughters, years ago when they were small, and I cry again as I read it to my mother.

You are not alone, I repeat. You'll live on, the way Charlotte does, through your grandchildren and their children. It's O.K. now. You can go.

As I put the book away, I see that her eyes are closed, finally, and that her breathing has evened out, so that it is shallow but calm.

It takes one more day. There are, it turns out, many different ways to help someone die.

SARAH LYALL is a writer at large for The New York Times, working for a variety of desks including Sports, Culture, Media and International. Previously she was a correspondent in the London bureau, and a reporter for the Culture and Metro Desks. She is the author of "The Anglo Files: A Field Guide to the British."

CHAPTER 4

Assisted Suicide Abroad

As America has struggled to determine its own policies on assisted suicide on a state-by-state basis, assisted suicide has gained more acceptance internationally, particularly in Europe. In the Netherlands, assisted suicide has been legalized and found mainstream acceptance, even for individuals without terminal illnesses. Meanwhile, cases in Italy and Australia have begun to receive national attention, resulting in the real possibility that assisted suicide might find its place in those countries as well.

A Poet Crusades for the Right to Die His Way

BY IAN FISHER | DEC. 20, 2006

ROME, DEC. 19 — Many patients on respirators are not conscious and so cannot say whether they want to live or die. But Piergiorgio Welby is still full of words, hard and touching ones, that may be changing the way Italy thinks about euthanasia and other choices for the sick to end their own lives.

"I love life, Mr. President," Mr. Welby, 60, who has battled muscular dystrophy for 40 years, wrote to Italy's president, Giorgio Napolitano, in September. "Life is the woman who loves you, the wind through your hair, the sun on your face, an evening stroll with a friend.

"Life is also a woman who leaves you, a rainy day, a friend who deceives you. I am neither melancholic nor manic-depressive. I find the idea of dying horrible. But what is left to me is no longer a life."

Now Mr. Welby's long drama appears to be nearing its final act. Last weekend, an Italian court denied legal permission for a doctor to sedate him and remove him from his respirator. Fully lucid but losing his capacity to speak and eat, he is deciding whether to appeal or to perform an act of civil disobedience that will kill him.

He is doing so in a very public way. Until a recent steep decline in his condition, he used a little stick to rapidly peck out blog entries with one hand. His book, "Let Me Die," was just released. Near daily front-page stories chronicle the political, ethical and, with the Catholic Church a vital force here, religious issues his case presents.

"Dear Welby: Wait Before Taking Yourself Off" the respirator, read a front-page headline on Tuesday in La Repubblica, written by a top Italian surgeon, Dr. Ignazio Marino, who is also a senator for the Democrats of the Left. He had visited Mr. Welby the day before.

What has given the case a particular political twist is that Mr. Welby, attached to a respirator for nine years, has long been a spokesman for euthanasia and is a central part of the Radical Party's effort to have it legalized. In fact, members of the Radical Party have offered to personally remove his respirator if asked — and may do so any day now in a frontal challenge to Italian law.

But the Catholic Church and many of this traditionally minded nation's politicians on the left and the right not only oppose euthanasia generally but are also not entirely sure what to do about Mr. Welby's case. He says he is not seeking to commit suicide but to remove himself from medical treatment he does not want.

"It is an unbearable torture," he wrote two weeks ago.

To decline forced medical treatment is allowed under Italian law, experts say, but Italy has another law that makes it a crime to assist in a death, even with consent. So a doctor could not detach the respirator without risking prosecution.

The church, too, has conflicting teachings about what to do in this case, and what the Vatican thinks has a deep impact not only on the nation's political class but also on doctors tied to the scores of Catholic-run hospitals around Italy.

The defense of life is central to the social doctrine of the church, and so it opposes abortion and capital punishment. Only last week Pope Benedict XVI reaffirmed his opposition to euthanasia, saying governments should find ways to let the terminally ill "face death with dignity."

The church also opposes medical treatments to artificially prolong life, but several church officials have worried recently that ending artificial life support could result in de facto euthanasia.

"The problem is to know if we find ourselves truly in front of a case of an artificial prolonging of life," Cardinal Javier Lozano Barragán, the Vatican's top official for health, said in a recent interview with La Repubblica.

Seeing the church as one major obstacle to dying as he wants to, Mr. Welby, a poet and prolific writer, has had little patience with the Vatican's argument for a "natural end" to life.

"What is natural about a hole in the belly and a pump that fills it with fats and proteins?" he wrote in his letter to the president. The letter was delivered with a video of Mr. Welby in his bed at his home in Rome attached in silence to the respirator, with a laptop at his bedside reading his words in a spooky synthesized voice.

"What is natural about a hole in the windpipe and a pump that blows air into the lungs?" he wrote. "What is natural about a body kept biologically functional with the help of artificial respirators, artificial feed, artificial hydration, artificial intestinal emptying, of death artificially postponed?"

The Radical Party, and to some extent Mr. Welby himself, have been criticized, largely from the political right, for turning the fight over his death into a political campaign. And certainly, experts say, scores of terminally ill patients end their lives in the way Mr. Welby wants to, though privately, and at the moment in Italy, illegally.

"If it is done privately, there would be a way to accommodate his desire to discontinue life support as a burdensome therapy," said Dr. Myles N. Sheehan, a Jesuit priest and physician at the Loyola University Medical Center in Chicago and an expert on ethical issues surrounding euthanasia. "But if it is done publicly, it's a big mess, because of the direct link to euthanasia."

Mr. Welby, in fact, wants to make his legacy erasing that ambiguity. He has been pushing for a broader law on euthanasia. He also sought a court ruling for a doctor to sedate him and detach him from the respirator, which several experts said would have given Italy a legal precedent in cases involving unwanted medical treatment.

Court rulings, the latest issued on Saturday, essentially acknowledged Mr. Welby's right to end medical treatment but did not allow a doctor to participate.

Still, his fight is having a political effect. Recent polls show a higher level of support among Italians for euthanasia. For the first time, there is a serious attempt in Parliament to pass a "living will" law that would allow Italians to declare what medical treatments they would accept.

Mr. Welby must now decide whether he wants to continue pursuing the legal track or whether he will die outside the law. Already Marco Cappato, a leader in the Radical Party and in a pro-euthanasia patients' group, said plans were being drawn up with Mr. Welby to end his life without a legal decision. "It's a very difficult moment for him," Mr. Cappato said. "The choice to die is not easy."

Italy to Allow Living Wills and the Refusal of End-of-Life Care

BY ELISABETTA POVOLEDO | DEC. 14, 2017

ROME — Italian lawmakers passed a law on Thursday allowing adults to decide, in concordance with their doctors, their end-of-life medical care, including the terms under which they can refuse treatment. The law permits Italians to write living wills and refuse medical treatment, artificial nutrition and hydration.

The bill had languished in Parliament for 30 years, facing strong resistance from conservative Catholic lawmakers, who presented more than 3,000 amendments to stymie its passage.

The amendments were rejected on Wednesday, before the final vote of 180 to 71.

This law was the result of grass-roots lobbying, "otherwise we would have never made it to the end," said Donata Lenzi, the lower house lawmaker who sponsored the bill through that chamber earlier this year, speaking to a small group of the law's supporters who had gathered to celebrate in front of the Italian Parliament on Thursday morning.

"This law does not take anything away from any ill person, this law gives," Ms. Lenzi said. "Because it recognizes that until the end you are not just a body to heal but a person with your own mind, your own ideas, your own convictions and you have the right to be heard."

Some lawmakers who opposed the law said it effectively introduced state-sanctioned euthanasia.

"It's a brutal chaos that doesn't cancel suffering but instead aggravates it," said Maurizio Gasparri, a member of the center-right Forza Italia party, during the debate in the Senate on Thursday. The law, he said, is confused from a legislative and constitutional point of view, and "profoundly wrong from an ethical and moral point of view," regardless of one's religious beliefs.

Pope Francis unexpectedly bolstered the prospects of the bill last month when he told participants at a medical conference in the Vatican that while euthanasia or assisted suicide was not permitted, stopping treatment for terminally ill people could in some cases be "morally licit" and "acknowledges the limitations of our mortality, once it becomes clear that opposition to it is futile."

"It is clear that not adopting, or else suspending, disproportionate measures means avoiding overzealous treatment," the pope said.

Determining the best course of action for a dying person requires interacting with the patient, the patient's family and doctors, because "the mechanical application of a general rule is not sufficient," he said.

Supporters of the bill used the pope's words to dismiss Catholic critics, noting that Francis had merely reiterated the longstanding teachings of the Roman Catholic Church when he said that its doctrine on the sanctity of life did not justify overzealous medical treatments to artificially prolong life.

Parliamentary debate also surged on momentum created by a headline-grabbing trial currently underway in a Milan courtroom. Marco Cappato, an activist, has been charged with "reinforcing the suicidal will" and assisting with arrangements for the suicide of Fabiano Antoniani, who died in a Swiss clinic on Feb. 28. He faces up to 12 years in prison.

Mr. Antoniani, a disc jockey known as D.J. Fabo, was left blind and paralyzed after a 2014 car accident. He breathed through a respirator, ate through a feeding tube and spoke with difficulty, though he remained lucid to the end.

In January, Mr. Antoniani posted a video appealing to President Sergio Mattarella to urge the government to pass a law allowing euthanasia. A popular television program, "Le Iene," championed his cause, producing several segments about Mr. Antoniani before and after his death in February.

A sentence is expected in mid-February.

For many right-to-die advocates, the law on living wills is a starting point for the infinitely tougher battle to allow terminally ill Italians to end their lives at home with medical support, rather than having to travel to countries where it is allowed.

Mr. Cappato has founded an association, Soccorso Civile, that provides information for terminally ill Italians. It has already helped three people go to Switzerland to end their lives and has received hundreds of requests for information, he said.

He and Mina Welby, the widow of Piergiorgio Welby, whose battle to end his life made headlines in 2006, are being investigated in the city of Massa Carrara in connection with the assisted suicide of Davide Trentini, who died in April.

"Every year the Italian state receives death certificates for 50 Italians" from towns in Switzerland that have clinics where assisted suicide is practiced, Mr. Cappato said in an interview this month.

"The Italian state knows what is going on but allows this to happen clandestinely," he said. "If I am acquitted, at least these trips could happen openly. But my objective is that medically assisted suicide and euthanasia become legal in Italy."

Also applauding the law's passage was Filomena Gallo, the national secretary of the Luca Coscioni right-to-die association. It has been a long series of "legal battles and suffering and then decisions that gave back the power to decide over one's own life," Ms. Gallo told supporters on Thursday.

She noted that a bill allowing euthanasia had gathered 67,000 signatures on a petition and had been submitted for discussion in the legislature but had not been addressed.

"We will propose it again in the next legislature," which will begin sessions after elections next year, she said.

"Now we know that battles for the freedom of persons can arrive at their objective."

Assisted Suicide of Healthy 79-Year-Old Renews German Debate on Right to Die

BY MARK LANDLER | JULY 3, 2008

FRANKFURT — When Roger Kusch helped Bettina Schardt kill herself at home on Saturday, the grim, carefully choreographed ritual was like that in many cases of assisted suicide, with one exception.

Ms. Schardt, 79, a retired X-ray technician from the Bavarian city of Würzburg, was neither sick nor dying. She simply did not want to move into a nursing home, and rather than face that prospect, she asked Mr. Kusch, a prominent German campaigner for assisted suicide, for a way out.

Her last words, after swallowing a deadly cocktail of the antimalaria drug chloroquine and the sedative diazepam, were "auf Wiedersehen," Mr. Kusch recounted at a news conference on Monday.

It was hardly the last word on her case, however. Ms. Schardt's suicide — and Mr. Kusch's energetic publicizing of it — have set off a national furor over the limits on the right to die, in a country that has struggled with this issue more than most because of the Nazi's euthanizing of at least 100,000 mentally disabled and incurably ill people.

"What Mr. Kusch did was particularly awful," Beate Merk, the justice minister of Bavaria, said in an interview. "This woman had nothing wrong other than her fear. He didn't offer her any other options."

Germany's conservative chancellor, Angela Merkel, declared on a German news channel on Wednesday, "I am absolutely against any form of assisted suicide, in whatever guise it comes."

On Friday, Bavaria and four other German states will push for new laws to ban commercial ventures that help people kill themselves. Suicide itself is not a crime, nor is aiding a suicide, provided it does not cross the line into euthanasia, or mercy killing.

But many here do not want Germany to follow the example of Switzerland, where liberal laws on euthanasia have led to a bustling trade in assisted suicide. In the last decade, nearly 500 Germans have crossed the border to end their lives with the help of a Swiss group that facilitates suicides.

"We want to make it illegal for people here to offer 'suicide by reservation,'" Ms. Merk said. "That is inhumane."

By helping Ms. Schardt end her life, and then broadcasting the result, Mr. Kusch has, in effect, hung out a shingle. A former senior government official from Hamburg, Mr. Kusch, 53, said he would help other people like her who decide of their own free will to commit suicide.

"My offer, since last Saturday, is to allow people to die in their own beds," he said in a telephone interview on Wednesday. "That is the wish of most people, and now it is possible in Germany."

With his penchant for brazen publicity, Mr. Kusch recalls Jack Kevorkian, the euthanasia crusader in Michigan who all but dared the authorities to stop his assisted suicides, and ended up in prison. But Mr. Kusch, who is trained as a lawyer, is careful not to cross the legal line.

In Ms. Schardt's case, he counseled her about how to commit suicide, but did not provide or administer the drugs. He left the room after she drank the poisonous brew and returned three hours later to find her dead on her bed. He videotaped the entire process as proof that he was not an active participant.

Prosecutors have looked into the case, but it does not appear that Mr. Kusch is in legal jeopardy.

Mr. Kusch also videotaped five hours of interviews with Ms. Schardt, in which she discussed her fears and why she wanted to die. He showed excerpts at the news conference, causing an outcry. "A 10-minute video says more than if I had talked for two hours," he said.

While Ms. Schardt was not suffering from a life-threatening disease, or in acute pain, her life was hardly pleasant, Mr. Kusch said. She had trouble moving around her apartment, where she lived alone.

Having never married, she had no family. She also had few friends, and rarely ventured out.

In such circumstances, a nursing home seemed likely to be the next stop. And for Ms. Schardt, who Mr. Kusch said feared strangers and had a low tolerance for those less clever than she was, that was an unbearable prospect.

"When she contacted me by e-mail on April 8, she had already decided to commit suicide," Mr. Kusch said, noting that she had also been in touch with Dignitas, the Swiss group that aids suicides.

In a goodbye letter to Mr. Kusch, posted on his Web site, Ms. Schardt thanked him, saying that if her death helped his battle it would fulfill her goal to have "the freedom to die in dignity."

To some champions of assisted suicide, Germany's laws do not allow for enough dignity. Ludwig A. Minelli, a former journalist who runs Dignitas, noted that those assisting in a suicide had to leave the person to die alone or risk being prosecuted. In Switzerland, he said, "the helping person, as well as family members or friends, could stay with the person who has decided to leave."

The larger lesson of Ms. Schardt's solitary death may have to do with the way Germany treats its old.

"The fear of nursing homes among elderly Germans is far greater than the fear of terrorism or the fear of losing your job," said Eugen Brysch, the director of the German Hospice Foundation. "Germany must confront this fear, because fear, as we have seen, is a terrible adviser."

Push for the Right to Die Grows in the Netherlands

BY DAVID JOLLY | APRIL 2, 2012

AMSTERDAM — It was 1989, and Dr. Petra de Jong, a Dutch pulmonologist, was asked for help by a terminally ill patient, a man in great pain with a large cancerous tumor in his trachea. He wanted to end his life.

She gave the man pentobarbital, a powerful barbiturate — but not enough. It took him nine hours to die.

"I realize now that I did things wrong," Dr. de Jong, 58, said in an interview in her office here. "Today you can Google it, but we didn't know."

Her warm and sincere manner belies, or perhaps attests to, her calling. The man was the first of 16 patients whom Dr. de Jong, now the head of the euthanasia advocacy group Right to Die-NL, has helped to achieve what she calls "a dignified death."

Founded in 1973, Right to Die-NL has been at the forefront of the movement to make euthanasia widely available in the Netherlands, even as the practice remains highly controversial elsewhere. Polls find that an overwhelming majority of the Dutch believe euthanasia should be available to suffering patients who want it, and thousands formally request euthanasia every year.

Right to Die-NL, which claims 124,000 members, made worldwide headlines in early March with the news that it was creating mobile euthanasia teams to help patients die at home. The organization has also courted controversy with its call for legislation to make euthanasia available to anyone over age 70, sick or not.

Dr. de Jong said more than 100 requests have been made for the mobile service. Several of them are being evaluated, and euthanasia has been performed in one case.

Advocates and critics of assisted suicide are watching the organization's efforts closely. Rick Santorum, the Republican presidential candidate from Pennsylvania, created something of a stir in February when he asserted — wrongly — that euthanasia accounted for 5 percent of all deaths in the Netherlands, and that many elderly Dutch wore wristbands that said "Do not euthanize me." Dutch officials quickly countered the claims.

"Internationally, the Dutch have pushed the conversation on both the wisdom of allowing people to choose how and when they die when they're in great suffering, and on the nature of compassion in dying," said Paul Root Wolpe, director of the Center for Ethics at Emory University in Atlanta.

Under the Netherlands' 2002 Termination of Life on Request and Assisted Suicide Act, doctors may grant patients' requests to die without fear of prosecution as long as they observe certain guidelines. The request must be made voluntarily by an informed patient who is undergoing suffering that is both lasting and unbearable. Doctors must also obtain the written affirmation of a second, independent physician that the case meets the requirements and report all such deaths to the authorities for review.

Dr. de Jong said Dutch physicians typically euthanize patients by injecting a barbiturate to induce sleep, followed by a powerful muscle relaxant like curare. For assisted suicide, the doctor prescribes a drug to prevent vomiting, followed by a lethal dose of barbiturates.

Almost 80 percent of all such deaths take place in patients' homes, according to the Royal Dutch Medical Association. In 2010, the latest year for which data are available, doctors reported 3,136 notifications of cases of "termination of life on request." Serious illnesses — late-stage cancer, typically — lie behind a vast majority.

Euthanasia is responsible for about 2 percent of all deaths annually in the Netherlands, according to Eric van Wijlick, a policy adviser for the association.

Euthanasia is typically carried out by the general practitioners who serve as the backbone of the country's universal health care system, doctors who often have enjoyed long relationships with their patients and know their feelings well. Mr. van Wijlick said the euthanasia law was possible because of "the moderate and open climate we have in the Netherlands, with respect for other points of view," and acknowledged that it would be difficult to carry out elsewhere, because everyone in the Netherlands has access to health care, an income and housing.

"There are no economic reasons to ask for euthanasia," he said, something that might not be true in the United States, with its for-profit health care system.

The mobile teams were needed, Dr. de Jong said, because many general practitioners, either for moral reasons or perhaps because of uncertainty about the law, refused to help suffering patients to die after it had become too late to find another doctor. The mobile teams will work to help them do so, she said.

Say a hypothetical 82-year-old man with metastasizing prostate cancer and poor prospects is told by his doctor that he does not qualify for euthanasia. The man could contact the Right to Die-NL's new "life-ending clinic," and if he appeared to meet the criteria, a doctor and a nurse would go to his home to make an assessment. If all the conditions were met, he would be euthanized, ideally with his family beside him.

Dr. de Jong emphasized that a patient could never be euthanized on the initial visit, because the law requires that a second physician be consulted.

Even in the Netherlands, some think Right to Die-NL may now be going too far. In addition to the mobile teams, the organization is among those pushing to give all people 70 years old and over the right to assisted death, even when they are not suffering from terminal illness. (The conservative government of Prime Minister Mark Rutte has said there will be no changes to the law under its tenure.)

"We think old people can suffer from life," Dr. de Jong said. "Medical technology is so advanced that people live longer and longer, and sometimes they say 'enough is enough.' "

Mr. Wijlick said the Royal Dutch Medical Association was "uneasy" with the mobile teams because "the question of euthanasia can't be taken out of isolation of the care of the patient," which should be in the hands of the primary caregiver, the general practitioner.

Most of the time, he added, there is a good reason that a doctor refuses euthanasia. Often, it is because the doctor believes the patient's case does not meet the criteria set out by law.

The association also opposes euthanasia for those "suffering from life." "There must always be a medical condition," Mr. van Wijlick said. Still, in such cases a doctor could explain to patients how to deny themselves food and drink, he noted, and could assist with any suffering that entailed.

The Dutch patients' organization N.P.V., a Christian group with 66,000 members, strongly criticizes the current application of the law, saying the practice of euthanasia has been extended to encompass patients with dementia and other conditions who may not by definition be competent to request help in dying.

Elise van Hoek-Burgerhart, a spokeswoman for the N.P.V., said in an e-mail that the idea of mobile euthanasia teams was "absurd," and that there was no way the mobile-team doctors could get to know a patient in just a few days. Moreover, she added, research shows that 10 percent of requests for euthanasia from the elderly would disappear if palliative care were better.

She also noted that the law requires review committees to sign off on every reported case of euthanasia, but that 469 cases from 2010 had still not been reviewed, meaning it was not clear how well doctors were adhering to the official guidelines.

Dr. Wolpe, the Emory University bioethicist, said he was "generally supportive" of people's right to choose their own death, but that he was troubled by some trends in the Netherlands, including the extension of euthanasia to people who were not suffering physically.

"When you switch from purely physiological criteria to a set of psychological criteria, you are opening the door to abuse and error," he said.

Dutch Law Would Allow Assisted Suicide for Healthy Older People

BY DAN BILEFSKY AND CHRISTOPHER F. SCHUETZE | OCT. 13, 2016

LONDON — In the Netherlands, a country vaunted for its liberalism, a proposal to legalize assisted suicide for older people who are generally healthy but feel they have led a full life has stirred up an ethical storm in some quarters.

In 2001, the Netherlands became the first country in the world to legalize euthanasia for patients who were suffering unbearable pain and had no prospects of a cure.

Now, some critics say the country has gone too far with a proposed law that would allow people who are not suffering from a medical condition to seek assisted suicide if they feel they have "completed life." Proponents of the law counter that limiting assisted death to patients with terminal illnesses is no longer enough, and that older people have the right to end their lives with dignity, and when they so choose.

Edith Schippers, the health minister, read a letter to the Dutch Parliament on Tuesday defending the measure. It is needed, she said, to address the needs of "older people who do not have the possibility to continue life in a meaningful way, who are struggling with the loss of independence and reduced mobility, and who have a sense of loneliness, partly because of the loss of loved ones, and who are burdened by general fatigue, deterioration and loss of personal dignity."

The letter said that the government of Prime Minister Mark Rutte hoped to draft the law by the end of 2017 in consultation with doctors and ethicists. It stressed that the law needed to be applied with great care, including careful vetting of potential applicants by a "death assistance provider" with a medical background.

While state-assisted suicide is deeply polarizing in many countries, including the United States, the practice has gained wide acceptance in the Netherlands. In 2015, euthanasia accounted for

5,516 deaths, or nearly 4 percent of all deaths in the country, a government agency says.

Nevertheless, there are opponents, and they say the latest proposal threatens to lead the country down a perilous moral and ethical path. They note that the proposal does not even cite a minimum age at which the law could be applied.

A populist politician, Geert Wilders, who has argued that Dutch tolerance on issues including immigration has gone too far, warned against the state acting as an enabler for the death of people who are lonely or depressed.

"We cannot allow people who are needy or lonely to be talked into dying," he told de Volkskrant, a leading Dutch newspaper. "Combating loneliness — and investing in dignity and focusing on our elderly — is always the best option."

Christian groups also lashed out against the proposed law, saying that it would encourage what they termed state-sanctioned murder.

"The myth is that it is purely individual choice, while it always also affects family, the community, health care providers and ultimately society," Gert-Jan Segers, the leader of a Christian parliamentary party, told de Volkskrant.

Some analysts said they believed the proposal was too vague, and cited concerns that some healthy older people might elect to end their lives out of fears of being a burden to their families.

The proposed law still faces several hurdles, including national elections next year that could change the composition of the government.

DAN BILEFSKY reported from London, and CHRISTOPHER F. SCHUETZE from
The Hague.

French Families Challenge Doctors on Wrenching End-of-Life Decisions

BY SCOTT SAYARE | JULY 31, 2014

PARIS — At least seven times, alone and in secret, Dr. Nicolas Bonne-maison prepared a lethal dose of sedative and quietly ended the life of a comatose patient in his care.

Dr. Bonnemaison, an emergency physician and palliative specialist in the city of Bayonne in southwestern France, acted without consul-tation of any kind — with other doctors, nurses or his dying patients' families — and sought to conceal the procedures, keeping them unre-corded. All this he admitted freely in court, saying he was moved by a sense of duty to act outside the law, to spare his colleagues and his patients' loved ones the strain of so weighty a choice. He was charged with the poisoning deaths of seven people.

"You wanted to protect everyone — the patients, the families, the medical personnel — out of compassion," a state prosecutor told Dr. Bonnemaison. "To be too compassionate is to deem others disposable. It is to unburden them of a responsibility that, in fact, belongs to them."

"I acted as a doctor," Dr. Bonnemaison told the court in June, "through to the very end."

A jury acquitted him. The courtroom, filled with his supporters, erupted in applause.

Doctors in France have long held what, by American standards, might seem unthinkable discretion to make end-of-life choices for peo-ple in their care.

For patients unable to communicate, such decisions fall legally to the physician, who may withdraw treatment or administer care that will end a patient's life so long as the stated intent is to relieve that patient's suffering, and not to kill. The opinions of family members and fellow doctors must be heard, the law states, but by no means obeyed.

That physicians wield such expansive powers is a peculiarity born of France's paternalistic bent, of a culture of deference to hierarchy and expertise, doctors and social scientists say. Never have fears of "death panels" become a matter of public debate, as they have in the United States.

As the population ages, however, and as drawn-out hospital deaths become more the norm, patients and families increasingly say they wish to be more closely involved in end-of-life decisions. And the French doctor's role as final arbiter of life and death is increasingly being challenged.

In June, a French high court for the first time heard a request to annul a doctor's decision to let a patient die. A bipartisan proposal for new end-of-life legislation is to be presented to President François Hollande in the coming months. And Dr. Bonnemaison's acquittal has been appealed by prosecutors.

"Here we're faced with someone who, because he's a doctor, is convinced of, inhabited by the notion that he must think in place of others, decide in place of others," said Dr. Régis Aubry, president of France's National Observatory on End of Life, a semiofficial organization that conducts research on end-of-life medical practices, speaking of Dr. Bonnemaison. "I find it chilling."

That traditional conception of the doctor's role has been undermined by an expansion in patient access to medical information, notably on the Internet, as well as technological advances and recent trends in care, doctors and researchers say. The movement to "tell the patient everything," for instance, which took hold decades ago in the United States, began far more recently in France, said Isabelle Baszanger, a sociologist who studies end-of-life care.

New circumstances, Dr. Aubry said, "are obliging us to adopt a much broader vision of the question of responsibility."

Demographic pressures are making end-of-life care a contentious moral, legal and economic issue in many countries. Aging populations and the growing costs of caring for them have left governments confronting trade-offs in policies affecting the closing weeks and months of life.

France's approach, codified in a 2005 law, is distinctly ambiguous. As nations across Europe have legalized euthanasia or assisted suicide in recent years, French lawmakers have publicly refused to do the same, often citing fears of misuse. Yet by empowering doctors with broad, discretionary end-of-life rights, France has in effect quietly authorized the practice of euthanasia, doctors and officials acknowledge.

About 57 percent of the 570,000 registered deaths in France in 2012 took place in a hospital, according to the national statistics agency, a level nearly twice that in the United States. A recent report by France's National Institute for Demographic Studies estimated that half of annual deaths were preceded by a doctor's decision to limit treatment or raise dosages of painkillers or sedatives.

Absent a stated desire to end a patient's suffering, the law bars doctors from intentionally ending a patient's life, whether by withholding treatment or administering a lethal dose of a drug, but such practices account for an estimated 3 percent of total deaths, or about 17,000 each year, the report said. In only one-fifth of those cases do doctors act at the explicit request of the patient. A major report on end-of-life practices prepared in 2012 for the French presidency found a generalized "deafness" among doctors toward their patients.

Much of the current debate in France has centered on the case of Vincent Lambert, who was paralyzed in a car crash six years ago and is now in a vegetative state. With the support of Mr. Lambert's wife, a doctor in the city of Reims has twice removed his feeding tube; twice, Mr. Lambert's parents, Roman Catholics who believe that their son's condition could yet improve, have won court injunctions to keep him alive.

Last month the case went before the Conseil d'État, France's highest administrative court, which found that Mr. Lambert, now 37, could legally be allowed to die; his parents have appealed that ruling to the European Court of Human Rights.

Before his accident, Mr. Lambert, a psychiatric nurse, said he did not wish to be kept alive if ever he were gravely injured, his wife and other relatives say. Given that, and after years of unsuccessful therapies, Mr. Lambert's medical team reasoned that to continue treating him would constitute "unreasonable obstinacy," which is discouraged under the 2005 law, said Dr. Éric Kariger, the lead doctor.

Before removing Mr. Lambert's feeding tube, however, Dr. Kariger failed to consult any members of the family, as required by law. Mr. Lambert's wife was later told of the doctor's decision; his parents discovered that the feeding tube had been removed in a visit to their son's bedside. They won an injunction, and the feeding tube was reinserted.

Dr. Kariger subsequently consulted Mr. Lambert's wife and parents, and once again removed the feeding tube.

"I told them, 'Hold on, it's not you making the decision — it's me,'" said Dr. Kariger. "Free yourselves of any feeling of guilt."

For many French, it is precisely because doctors are professionals, bound by medical and legal principles — not, in theory, by emotion or subjective experience — that they should be charged with making end-of-life decisions. François Lambert, Vincent's nephew and a plaintiff in the case who would like to let his uncle die, cited the deep divisions within his own family as proof of the need for a third-party decider.

The 2005 legislation is built upon the same conclusion, said Dr. Jean Leonetti, a cardiologist and lawmaker who saw the law through Parliament. Families might be guided by "too much emotion," Dr. Leonetti said.

The notion that patients themselves should be closely involved in medical decisions has come recently to France. Since 2002, for instance, patients have been legally entitled to gain access to their medical files without their doctor's consent. Many doctors maintain that patients ought not to be kept fully informed.

"One must not traumatize people," Dr. Leonetti said. "It's not worth going to knock on the door to say, 'You have 15 days to live' if the patient isn't asking for it, if he's not insisting on it. I don't see why one would snuff out any little lights of hope."

At the trial of Dr. Bonnemaison, several doctors admitted they had intentionally ended patients' lives. No charges have been brought against them.

"Traditionally, the doctor has been a man who acts alone," Ms. Baszanger said. "We know we're at the end of a system."

Justin Trudeau Seeks to Legalize Assisted Suicide in Canada

BY IAN AUSTEN | APRIL 14, 2016

OTTAWA — The government of Prime Minister Justin Trudeau introduced legislation on Thursday to legalize physician-assisted suicide for Canadians with a "serious and incurable illness," which has brought them "enduring physical or psychological suffering."

The proposed law limits physician-assisted suicides to citizens and residents who are eligible to participate in the national health care system, an effort to prevent a surge in medical tourism among the dying from other countries.

If the bill passes, Canada will join a group of countries that permit some form of assisted suicide, including Belgium, the Netherlands, Switzerland and Germany. Assisted suicide is legal in only a few American states, including Oregon and Vermont.

Under Canada's proposed law, people who have a serious medical condition and want to die will be able to commit suicide with medication provided by their doctors or have a doctor or nurse practitioner administer the dose for them. Family members and friends will be allowed to assist patients with their death, and social workers and pharmacists will be permitted to participate in the process.

The legislation is the latest step in a decades-long and frequently emotional debate in Canada about the rights and protections of patients with serious medical conditions who might seek to end their lives.

The legislation is expected to pass, given the Liberal Party's strong majority in the House of Commons. However, the government has promised to further study the issue after the law's passage and may make changes to the system.

"For some, medical assistance in dying will be troubling," Jody Wilson-Raybould, the justice minister, said at a news conference on Thursday. "For others, this legislation will not go far enough."

The bill would allow consenting adults "capable of making decisions with respect to their health" to choose to end their own lives or seek assistance in doing so from their doctors. A physician must decide that "natural death has become reasonably foreseeable, taking into account all of their medical circumstances."

Officials said that a patient does not have to have a terminal condition, citing the example of someone with an immune system deficiency which leaves them vulnerable to lethal infections.

Two independent physicians must agree and the patient must wait 15 days before moving to end his or her life, though the bill would allow for that waiting period to be shortened under certain circumstances.

Doctors will not be required to help people die, but they must refer patients to another physician if they have an objection to participating.

"I've seen people die well and I've seen people die in misery," Dr. Jane Philpott, the health minister who is also a family physician, told reporters on Thursday after the bill was introduced. "I want Canadians to have access to the best care possible."

The government's proposal is more restrictive than some proponents of legal assisted suicide had sought. It does not include provisions for minors who may be capable of making decisions about their own medical care to choose to end their lives, nor does it allow for people in the early stages of illnesses like dementia to request an assisted death while they are still competent.

"This law actually pits me against medical ethics," said Dr. Brett Belchetz, a physician with Dying With Dignity Canada, an advocacy group. "There are a number of shortfalls and I do think the legislation requires an urgent rethink."

Critics of the legislation, including some religious groups, have long opposed any form of assisted death.

"It changes our approach to human life, it changes our approach to human society," Cardinal Thomas Collins, the Roman Catholic Archbishop of Toronto, said in an interview Thursday after the new bill was introduced. He added that he was "deeply troubled" by the pressure the legislation might put on health care workers who object to assisted suicide.

Mr. Trudeau, who came to power in the fall, moved to introduce the bill to fill the legal void left in February 2015 when the Supreme Court of Canada overturned a criminal ban on assisted suicide.

The court had unanimously concluded that it was unconstitutional to deny the option of assisted death to consenting adults with severe medical conditions. At that time, the previous government, led by Stephen Harper, had one year to introduce a new law.

But Mr. Harper's Conservative Party was divided on the issue and did little to introduce legislation before last October's election.

When it became apparent that the Conservative government was not going to act on the court's ruling, the province of Quebec used its powers over health care to introduce a system for assisted dying late last year. Judges in other parts of Canada have also given individual patients permission to hasten their own deaths.

The previous government, backed by some religious leaders, vigorously challenged any attempts to legalize assisted suicide through the courts.

Mr. Trudeau, before he became prime minister, had supported a law that would allow for doctor-aided deaths, a position he said was informed by the final days before the death of his father, former Prime Minister Pierre Elliott Trudeau. He died in 2000 after declining aggressive treatments for prostate cancer and Parkinson's disease.

A few Liberal members of Parliament in Mr. Trudeau's party have said that the new law conflicts with their religious beliefs, and they will not support the legislation. Still, the bill is expected to pass but maybe not by June 6, the date on which the current criminal prohibition expires.

Michael Cooper, a Conservative member of Parliament, said his party will work with the government to make sure that the deadline is met.

Mr. Cooper said that he was pleased that the legislation proposes a narrower system than the one put forward this year by a parliamentary committee, though he added that he is still opposed to using nurse practitioners to aid assisted deaths.

Dominic LeBlanc, the Liberal Party leader in the House of Commons, told reporters Thursday that he would propose extended parliamentary sessions to pass the legislation in time.

He also reminded opponents of the bill that "this question of whether Canadians should have access or not was decided by a unanimous Supreme Court." Defeating or delaying the legislation beyond the June deadline, he said, would leave "a complete vacuum."

Was a Scientist's Death Murder or an 'Act of Mercy'?

BY RICK ROJAS | AUG. 28, 2018

BUNDANOON, AUSTRALIA — Even into her 80s, Mary E. White thrived on the expanse of Australian rain forest she had made her home, and she told friends of ambitious plans: She was going to write her autobiography, and there were two other books she wanted to finish.

But dementia robbed her of vigor. Ms. White, an accomplished scientist who gained prominence for warnings of desert encroachment and overpopulation, soon moved into a nursing home closer to her family but far from her old home. She could not communicate, friends said, and did not recognize visitors.

Then, one evening this month, Ms. White was found dead. She was 92. Several days later, her daughter was charged with murdering her.

The accusations have stunned people who knew Ms. White and her family, as well as Bundanoon, the small town where neighbors remembered an attentive daughter who would take her mother to the salon for haircuts and stop in the cafe across the street. Many insist that whatever happened must have been motivated by compassion and love.

"It would have been done as an act of mercy," said Jenny Goldie, a friend who had known Ms. White for 30 years. "There wouldn't have been any malice attached to it at all."

The case has saddened and confused Ms. White's friends. But it has also tapped into the broader debate in Australia over euthanasia and assisted dying, which has been renewed in recent weeks as Parliament considered a proposal to overturn a two-decade-old ban on the practice in the nation's territories.

The legislation ultimately failed, but last year, the state of Victoria became the first in Australia to legalize assisted dying, allowing someone with an incurable illness and limited life expectancy to obtain a dose of a lethal drug, and other states are considering their own

Australian lawmakers reacting last year in the state of Victoria's Parliament after a bill legalizing assisted dying was enacted.

legislation. (The Victoria law requires that a patient be mentally sound enough to make the request on his or her own, preventing relatives or caretakers from applying on an ill person's behalf.)

No such allowance exists in New South Wales, where Bundanoon sits a two-hour drive southwest of Sydney; an assisted dying bill was rejected last year.

Some have viewed Ms. White's case as an example of why that conversation must continue.

It has already stirred a delicate discussion about the toll of aging and illness, as well as the impact of watching a family member's decline. It is a subject that especially resonates in Bundanoon, where the population tends to skew older. (The median age, according to census figures, is 56.)

Just over 2,700 people live in Bundy, as Bundanoon is known. It's a rural outpost set back on country roads winding through vast golden fields specked with horses and sheep. The last time the town attracted widespread notice was nearly a decade ago, when residents voted to ban the sale of bottled water.

Violence of any kind is rare. "Stuff like that never happens in Bundy," said Olivia Cole, who has lived here for much of her life, referring to the murder charge that has rattled the community. "Nothing happens. No crime happens."

Some have acknowledged that they could recognize themselves and their parents in Ms. White's case. The authorities have indicated that the family had asked at her nursing home about euthanasia, and many here suspect that as Ms. White's health declined, her daughter, Barbara Eckersley, must have felt compelled to intervene.

"It stopped the mother's suffering," said Peter Giannakos, who has owned the Primula Cafe and Restaurant on the town's main street for 25 years.

Some of his customers said such an act could be justifiable. He considered his own mother-in-law, who is 96 and infirm, and said he was less certain.

"I can't do it," he said. "I can't do it."

Ms. White, who was found dead at the nursing home, was killed on the evening of Aug. 5, the police said, and Ms. Eckersley was arrested on Aug. 8. Local news reports said a lethal combination of medications had caused Ms. White's death.

Ms. Eckersley, 66, has been released on bail. Through her lawyer, she declined to comment, as did other family members. Friends said the two women had been close. Among other things, they shared an interest in science.

Ms. White, who did not often discuss her religious beliefs with friends, described having a spiritual connection with nature, which was her life's work.

She was born in southern Africa, in what is now Zimbabwe, and she studied paleobotany at the University of Capetown. She moved with her husband, a geologist, and their children to Australia in 1955.

While working as a research associate for the Australian Museum in Sydney, she assembled a plant fossil collection that included 12,000 specimens. Sometimes when her husband was sent to Northern Australia for government work he would send home drums filled with fossils for Ms. White to study.

Over time, her writing evolved from largely academic texts to books, with titles like "Listen … Our Land is Crying" and "Running Down: Water in a Changing Land," that denounced unsustainable land and water use in Australia and the threats posed by a booming population.

These were the works that became her legacy. "Mary White's contribution to our understanding of the natural cycles that drive all life on the planet and of our human impact on those processes is unsurpassed," Chrissie Goldrick, the editor in chief of Australian Geographic, said in a statement.

In 2003, Ms. White bought the sprawling property called Falls Forest, a four-hour drive up the coast from Sydney. Conservationists praised her for sparing some 200 acres of forest and preserving its biodiversity and for opening it to the public. She identified and labeled the plants along pathways around the property. Platypus were sometimes spotted in the creek near the house, where wallabies and eastern gray kangaroos routinely hopped by.

"It was Mary's concern that we were losing too many of these ancient forests," said Brett Dolsen, a photographer who befriended Ms. White and made a short documentary film about her. "Mary's work will never be forgotten in scientific and educational fields," he said, describing much of her work as pioneering. "Her message to humanity is what she lived for in protecting our planet."

Mr. Dolsen spent much time with Ms. White at Falls Forest, often sitting with her on the veranda, where she would take the cover off her parrot's cage, wishing the bird a good morning and insisting Mr. Dolsen do the same.

He was astonished by her energy. At 88, he said, she still ran the property, with its conference center and villas for guests. But he learned that her increasingly methodical approach to life was a way of navigating her dementia.

"Mary had forewarned me that her memory was failing," he said, "and that there were certain protocols I would need to know, including our arrangements and times for meeting."

By the time she left the property a few years ago and moved to Bundanoon, where her daughter lives, the disease had accelerated considerably. Ms. Goldie said that Ms. White's family had told her that she was essentially incapacitated. "She was the diametric opposite of what she had been before," Ms. Goldie said.

Ms. Goldie, who had gotten to know Ms. White through their involvement in environmental advocacy, had visited Ms. Eckersley's home about a week before Ms. White died. Ms. Goldie said she sensed tension.

"No smiling," she said. "No laughter in the house."

She recognized the strain Ms. Eckersley was under. She was reminded of the anguish she faced as her mother's health declined. It wasn't clear if prosecutors pursuing the murder charge would take such issues into account, but they had not yet suggested any ulterior motive in Ms. White's death.

"It's just very hard when you have to sort of encounter it every day," Ms. Goldie said. "They knew I understood and I think they appreciated that. But I don't think I understood how desperate Barbara must have been."

Why David Goodall, 104, Renowned Australian Scientist, Wants to Die

BY YONETTE JOSEPH | MAY 3, 2018

DAVID GOODALL, 104, an accomplished Australian scientist, isn't terminally ill, but he wants to die.

Mr. Goodall says his quality of life has deteriorated so badly that he has no reason to live, and he would like to end his life through assisted suicide. But he can't do it in his own country, where the practice is banned.

So on Wednesday, he took what was expected to be his last flight, bound for Europe, to accomplish his goal — and his quest has renewed a debate in Australia about the right to end one's life and what role others should play.

Mr. Goodall left his home in Perth to fly to an assisted-dying agency in Basel, Switzerland, a country where assisted suicide has been allowed for decades.

Though nations like Belgium, Canada, Colombia, Luxembourg and the Netherlands (along with some American states and the District of Columbia) permit euthanasia or assisted suicide, Switzerland is the only country with centers that offer assisted-suicide services to foreigners if the person assisting acts unselfishly.

When Mr. Goodall, a renowned ecologist, turned 104 in April, he told the Australian broadcaster ABC, "I greatly regret having reached that age."

Asked if he was happy, he responded: "I'm not happy. I want to die. It's not sad particularly. What is sad is if one is prevented."

At the airport on Wednesday, Mr. Goodall expressed regret at having to leave Australia to fulfill his wish, telling reporters, "I'm sorry that I have to travel to Switzerland in order to execute it."

Sitting in a wheelchair, he added: "I've lived quite a good life until recently. The last year has been less satisfactory for me because I couldn't do things."

Philip Nitschke, a right-to-die activist and author whose organization, Exit International, helped Mr. Goodall pay for his plane ticket in business class through a GoFundMe campaign, said on Twitter: "Australia will not allow him to access the drugs to achieve this, but Switzerland does."

He added, "The world is changing but Australia lags badly."

Assisted suicide has been banned in Australia for decades. In 1995, the Northern Territory became the first legislature in the world to pass a law for voluntary euthanasia, but it was overturned by the national Parliament in 1997.

Victoria State passed a bill in 2017 to legalize assisted suicide, but it could not benefit Mr. Goodall. Set to go into effect in June 2019, it will apply only to terminally ill patients who are of sound mind and who have a life expectancy of no more than six months.

The Australian Medical Association is generally strongly opposed to assisted dying. "Doctors are not trained to kill people. It is deep within our ethics, deep within our training that that's not appropriate," its president, Dr. Michael Gannon, said during a legislative debate in Victoria last year.

"Not every doctor agrees with that," he allowed.

Indeed, a survey of the A.M.A. found that four in 10 members supported right-to-die policies, according to the BBC.

Mr. Goodall, who was born in Britain, began his scientific career at Imperial College in London, according to Exit International. At the University of Melbourne, he was a senior lecturer and held positions at what is now the University of Ghana; the University of Reading, England; the University of California; and Utah State University, among other institutions.

Having earned three doctorates, he worked with the Commonwealth Scientific and Industrial Research Organization, an independent Australian government agency, until his semiretirement in 1979. He was awarded the Order of Australia at age 101.

Mr. Goodall lived alone in his later years, though he has children and several grandchildren. Most of his friends have died. But he did his own shopping, read Shakespeare and presented poetry to a group.

Until 2016, he worked as an honorary research associate at the Center for Ecosystem Management at Edith Cowan University in Perth, taking two buses and a train to get to his office four days a week.

When he was 102 and called Australia's oldest working scientist, the university stirred up a tempest by asking Mr. Goodall to vacate his office on the grounds that he was too frail and a safety risk to himself. He challenged the decision, but he moved closer to home to continue working.

His world became smaller, however, as he was forced to give up driving and performing in the theater, Carol O'Neill, a friend and a representative of Exit International, told the BBC.

"It was just the beginning of the end," she said.

Then, last month, he fell in his one-bedroom apartment and was not found for two days. Doctors ordered him not to use public transport or even to cross the road by himself. His physical condition deteriorated.

His daughter, Karen Goodall-Smith, a clinical psychologist, told ABC at his party that his work had probably been keeping him alive. "His work is his hobby, as well as his passion," she said, "and without his work, I don't think that there would be a purpose for him any more."

Ms. Goodall-Smith added, according to Exit: "He has no control over his life, over his body, over his eyesight. He has lived a really good 104 years. Whatever happens, whatever choices are made, they're up to him."

Mr. Goodall is adamant. "One should be free to use the rest of one's life as one chooses," he has said. "If one chooses to kill oneself, then that's fair enough. I don't think anyone else should interfere."

According to ABC, he is expected to succumb next Thursday.

David Goodall, 104, Scientist Who Fought to Die on His Terms, Ends His Life

BY YONETTE JOSEPH AND ILIANA MAGRA | MAY 10, 2018

LONDON — On the eve of his death, David Goodall, 104, Australian scientist, father, grandfather and right-to-die advocate, was asked if he had any moments of hesitation, "even fleeting ones."

"No, none whatever," Mr. Goodall said in a strong voice. "I no longer want to continue life, and I'm happy to have a chance tomorrow to end it."

Mr. Goodall spoke on Wednesday before a phalanx of journalists and photographers in Basel, Switzerland. That the inquisitors had come from around the globe to hear what would be most likely the last public words of the man once called Australia's oldest working scientist was evidence that his campaign to end his life had captivated audiences worldwide.

On Thursday, Mr. Goodall died about 12:30 p.m. local time, according to Exit International, a right-to-die organization of which he had been a longtime member.

A botanist and ecologist of some renown, he was not terminally ill, but his health had deteriorated so badly that he had to stop most of his activities — like working at Edith Cowan University in Perth and performing in the theater — and he did not want to continue living. A fall in his home last month exacerbated his condition.

Keenly aware that the news conference on Wednesday was one last opportunity to help promote euthanasia and assisted dying in his own country, Mr. Goodall withstood the barrage of questions, squinting because of the flashing cameras and sometimes struggling to understand because of his hearing loss.

He was flanked by Philip Nitschke, the director of Exit International, and Moritz Gall, a representative for Lifecircle, an association that supports people going through major life decisions and guides them through the laws of Switzerland.

Mr. Goodall said, "I've had a good life." He was not afraid of death but acknowledged that he previously tried to end his life in Australia.

"It would've been much more convenient for everyone if I had been able to," he said, "but unfortunately it failed."

He was crystal clear about why he had chosen "the Swiss option." Euthanasia and assisted dying are banned in Australia, though Victoria State has passed a law on assisted dying that goes into effect next year; it will apply only to terminally ill patients who have a life expectancy of no more than six months.

He said he hoped his life story would "increase the pressure" on Australia to change its laws. "One wants to be free to choose his death when death is at the appropriate time," Mr. Goodall said.

He had flown to Basel from his home in Perth last week with the help of Exit International and entered an assisted-dying center on Monday. Lifecircle, which works with the Eternal Spirit, a foundation that facilitates assisted voluntary death, helped him navigate the process. He had consultations this week with two doctors, including a psychiatrist, in Switzerland, and was visited by the Swiss police as a formality.

On Wednesday, realizing that his case had ricocheted around the world and that responding to the outpouring of requests for interviews would have consumed all of his last few days, Mr. Goodall consented to one final news conference.

He expressed gratitude to the Swiss and regret at having to leave home for Switzerland, the only country that offers assisted-dying services to foreigners if the person assisting does not benefit from the person's death. (Only 40 Australians are known to have made the journey, according to Exit International, because of the length of the flight and the cost of the trip.)

"I am very appreciative of the hospitality of the Swiss Federation and the ability that one has here to come to an end gracefully," Mr.

Goodall said, adding, "I greatly regret that Australia is behind Switzerland in this move."

He said that no one in his family had pressured him to change his mind. As for leaving his children and grandchildren behind, he said: "I have already said my piece to my family. I send them my love and I'm glad that I had the opportunity of seeing most of them for the past week."

Asked if there was anything he still wanted to do, he said: "There are many things I would like to do, of course, but it's too late. I'm content to leave them undone."

Pressed about what he would miss, he allowed, "I have been missing for a long time my journeys into the Australian countryside, but I haven't been able to do that for quite a while."

He was asked about his last meal. "I'm rather limited in my culinary enjoyment nowadays," he responded. "I don't find that I can enjoy my meals as I used to."

On Thursday, he received a fatal dose of a barbiturate intravenously. In order to comply with Swiss law that bans the interference of third parties in the process, he opened the valve to release the solution himself and fell asleep, dying soon after. Some of his grandchildren were with him in his final hours, Exit International said.

He wanted no funeral and no remembrance service, and he asked that his body be donated to medicine or his ashes sprinkled locally, according to Exit. Mr. Goodall did not believe in the afterlife, the organization said.

How would he like to be remembered? "As an instrument of freeing the elderly from the need to pursue their life irrespective," he said at the news conference on Wednesday.

At one point, he was asked what tune he would choose for his last song, and he said the final movement of Beethoven's Ninth Symphony. Then he began to sing, with verve and vigor.

According to Mr. Nitschke, Mr. Goodall did end up choosing Beethoven, and he died the moment "Ode to Joy" concluded.

CHAPTER 5

Reaching the End

In this final chapter, Catherine Porter tells the story of John Shields, a Canadian man who decided to schedule his own wake following a diagnosis of amyloidosis. In this tremendous piece of reporting, Porter documents the details of his final days, which were made possible by Canada's end of life laws. This longform profile shows how control over the end of his life allowed Shields to create an extraordinary death for himself.

At His Own Wake, Celebrating Life and the Gift of Death

BY CATHERINE PORTER | MAY 25, 2017

Tormented by an incurable disease, John Shields knew that dying openly and without fear could be his legacy, if his doctor, friends and family helped him.

VICTORIA, BRITISH COLUMBIA — Two days before he was scheduled to die, John Shields roused in his hospice bed with an unusual idea. He wanted to organize an Irish wake for himself. It would be old-fashioned with music and booze, except for one notable detail — he would be present.

The party should take up a big section of Swiss Chalet, a family-style chain restaurant on the road out of town. Mr. Shields wanted his last supper to be one he so often enjoyed on Friday nights when he was a young Catholic priest — rotisserie chicken legs with gravy.

Then, his family would take him home and he would die there in the morning, preferably in the garden. It was his favorite spot, rocky and wild. Flowering native shrubs pressed in from all sides and a stone

Buddha and birdbath peeked out from among the ferns and boulders. Before he got sick, Mr. Shields liked to sit in his old Adirondack chair and watch the bald eagles train their juveniles to soar overhead. He meditated there twice a day, among the towering Douglas firs.

"Someone once asked me how did I get to become unique," he said that afternoon in his hospice bed. "I recommend meditation as a starting place — bringing your consciousness to bear."

Mr. Shields intended to die swiftly and peacefully by lethal injection, administered by his doctor. Last June, the Canadian government legalized what it termed "medical assistance in dying" for competent adult patients who are near death and suffering intolerably from irremediable illnesses. When his doctor, Stefanie Green, informed him that he qualified, Mr. Shields felt the first hope since a doctor told him more than a year before that he had a rare and incurable disease called amyloidosis, which caused proteins to build up in his heart and painfully damage the nerves in his arms and legs.

Having control over the terms of his death made him feel empowered over the disease rather than crippled by it, a common response among Dr. Green's patients. Mr. Shields believed that dying openly and without fear could be his most meaningful legacy — which was saying something. The man had packed five lifetimes of service into one: He had been a civil rights activist, a social worker for children, the head of British Columbia's biggest union and, most recently, the savior of a floundering land trust that included 7,191 acres of protected wilderness and historic properties.

His newly developed plan for how he would spend his last moments, though, worried his wife, Robin June Hood. Her husband had not left his bed once since he arrived at the hospice on a stretcher, 17 days earlier. His 78-year-old body had thinned; his voice dimmed. He lasted only 15 minutes in conversation before his eyes fluttered closed. Just leaving the room would exhaust him. She knew he could not make it to the restaurant, and there was no way she could tend to his needs at home, even for one night — especially his last.

John Shields.

Happily, Dr. Green had become adept at brokering delicate family discussions over the past year. She had presided over 35 deaths since the law passed, each intimately different from the next. One man got dressed in his amateur clown costume, complete with wig and red nose, and died telling her jokes. He had insisted on being alone in the room with her, but most of her patients died surrounded by loved ones. Many were too sick to devise elaborate rituals, but others had chosen the location, attendees, readings and music as if planning a wedding. Dr. Green called them something she picked up at a conference on euthanasia in the Netherlands: "choreographed deaths."

She arrived at Mr. Shields's hospice room that day to finalize the plans. The couple held hands as she helped them stitch a compromise. On March 23, the last night of Mr. Shields's life, they would host a party in the hospice solarium with Swiss Chalet takeout for all. The next morning, he would die in his hospice room. Then, his wife and stepdaughter would take his body home and lay it out in his beloved garden for two days.

The plan, Mr. Shields said that afternoon, was "absolutely terrific."

ONE MAN'S COSMIC JOURNEY

A year and a half earlier, Mr. Shields was driving down a wooded provincial highway across the belly of Vancouver Island when he blacked out. His S.U.V. crossed the centerline, plunged into a ditch and hit a tree.

Ms. Hood, who had been sleeping in the back seat, was violently thrown. She snapped five ribs and ruptured her spleen. Mr. Shields broke his back in three places. When he came to, he thought he had been paralyzed.

The fact that he was not, and that they had not been killed or struck another car, seemed a sign to Mr. Shields. Then there was this: An off-duty firefighter or police officer (they cannot remember which) happened to be driving behind them and summoned rescue workers, who arrived within minutes. Even their little cairn terrier, Diego, was rushed to emergency surgery.

Mr. Shields believed every person played a part in the continuing evolution of the universe. Clearly, he thought, he had more to do.

But just a few months later, in the fall of 2015, a doctor summoned him to his office and broke the news. A biopsy of his heart, taken after the accident, revealed that Mr. Shields had a hereditary form of amyloidosis. The disease had caused his heart to stop temporarily — hence his blacking out behind the wheel — and was the source of the numbness and painful tingling in his fingers and feet that had plagued him for a couple of years.

The disease was unpredictable, but it would likely cause him to lose all feeling and basic use of his arms and legs before shutting down his heart, Mr. Shields recalled the doctor's telling him.

Mr. Shields had seen a friend die from a painful and disabling disease. He was terrified of facing a similar fate. "One quality of life that's important to me is my dignity — and sparing anxiety for my wife and daughter," he said. Becoming debilitated and being tube-fed was unacceptable to him. "All of those painful and demeaning things," he said, "I considered beyond the threshold of how I would like to live."

If service was the biggest theme of Mr. Shields's life, the other was freedom — intellectual, spiritual, personal. He was always growing and exploring. In the last few months of his life, he tried a psychedelic drug for the first time and enrolled in an advanced online course on "transcending transpersonal realms."

Mr. Shields was the rare combination of introspective extrovert. He could be seen wearing a silly hat made from a napkin one night and hosting a spiritual circle for men on another.

He loved rituals, which began with the Catholic Masses of his childhood in New York City. He was the only child of a steamfitter and a teacher, both Irish and devout. Family lore had it that when Mr. Shields was a baby, his grandfather hoisted him up in one hand and proclaimed he would be America's first pope.

At 17, he enrolled in seminary. By the time he was ordained years later, the Second Vatican Council had convened. Shaken at first by changes the council was recommending, Mr. Shields came to embrace them, especially the use of modern historical criticism in interpreting Scripture.

In his mind, this changed Christ's message from one of sin's redemption to pure love. But his was a minority view, and it set him on a radical path at odds with his bosses. He was transferred from his first parish, in Vancouver, and then barred from preaching and teaching at his second posting, in Austin, Tex., after he challenged the pope's opposition to birth control.

After only four years, he walked away from the priesthood, forlorn and distressed. The decision cost him not only his faith, but also his purpose and livelihood.

But from that difficult time emerged two loves. One was Madeleine Longo, who had worked with him in both places and who soon became his wife. The second was the wild and rugged landscapes of British Columbia, Vancouver's province.

In 1969, the couple moved here and Mr. Shields found a job as a social worker. His first clients were unwed pregnant women, many of whom wanted illegal abortions. He put aside any vestiges of Catholic doctrine after he heard their anguished stories. For Mr. Shields, nothing was black and white.

He eventually became a manager, but was not satisfied treating problems at what he called the "discharge end of the social injustice pipe." As a seminary student, he was active in the civil rights movement and had met the Rev. Dr. Martin Luther King Jr.

He wanted transformational change.

Mr. Shields successfully ran for president of the British Columbia Government Employees' Union — which over his 14-year tenure grew by more than 20,000 members to around 58,700. He was known as "the skipper" — a calm captain who was open-minded and unerringly ethical, but also tough. He was most proud of securing equal pay for women in the union.

While his post-church professional life surged with purpose, Mr. Shields's search for existential and spiritual answers was slow and meandering, often veering to the fringe.

He studied Gestalt therapy and picked up dowsing, the art of divining energy with copper rods. Finally, a lecture by Brian Swimme, a professor at the California Institute of Integral Studies, changed Mr. Shields's life. He became a spiritual cosmologist, believing that the universe was conscious and that everything was inextricably connected.

"We come out of the universe to play a role in the unfolding of the universe," Mr. Shields wrote in his 2011 memoir, "The Priest Who Left His Religion in Pursuit of Cosmic Spirituality." "This perspective riveted me. This is the opposite of meaningless. I come forth at this precise moment to contribute my unique gifts to the great unfolding."

In 1999, when Ms. Longo became ill with lymphoma, Mr. Shields decided to step down from his union post and care for her full time.

He was still grieving from her death, in 2005, when he met Ms. Hood, an environmentalist with a doctorate in education who was 15 years his junior and had spent years working on human rights in Central America.

She moved into his daffodil-colored stucco house, at the base of a cliff. It seemed more a cabin in a national park than a home in an old and genteel part of Victoria locally referred to as "behind the tweed curtain." Deer grazed on bushes nearby and raccoons wandered liberally, enticed by the bowls of food and water set out by Mr. Shields. Orcas could be seen in the ocean, just a block away, and beyond that the white-capped peaks of Washington State's Olympic Peninsula.

Ms. Hood's then-19-year-old daughter, Nikki Sanchez, joined them and developed a close bond with Mr. Shields. Later, he would refer to her simply as his daughter and write that her love was "one of the most delicious gifts of a generous universe."

Ms. Hood warned him that marrying her also meant inheriting a tribe of female friends she called "the intertidals." Over the years, many would wash up on their doorstep after a storm, and move in for weekends or longer.

One, an environmentalist and writer, Briony Penn, had persuaded Mr. Shields to come out of semiretirement and help steer The Land Conservancy, which was heavily in debt. He was driving home from a conservancy meeting the day he blacked out and crashed his car.

After the diagnosis, Mr. Shields retreated into his study and fell into the throes of grief. As someone who treasured independence, the concept of being trapped in his own body frightened him. He searched on the internet for what he called "life-ending cocktails."

FROM BIRTH TO DEATH: A DOCTOR'S GIFT

Three walls of Stefanie Green's office are collaged with the faces of hundreds of smiling, angelic-looking newborns that she delivered over her 22-year career.

Until three years ago, she specialized in maternity and newborn care with a side practice in circumcisions — which started not because of her Jewish upbringing but because few local doctors were willing to perform them.

To her, it was a matter of principle. "It's about choice — the same as MAID," said Dr. Green, a 48-year-old mother of two, referring to the medical assistance in dying law. "Give people good information and let them do what they think is best for their family."

Dr. Green gives off the aura of a university volleyball team captain — warm, competent, no frills, no makeup, nothing hidden. Last year, she took bridge lessons with a group of octogenarians at the local seniors' center and now plays weekly.

For family reasons, she took time off and decided she needed a better life-work balance than the erratic schedule of delivering babies allowed. A month before the new law came into effect, she traveled to the Netherlands for a conference on euthanasia.

"Birth and death, deliveries in and out — I find it very transferable," she explained one morning as she walked her small white poodle, Benji, on a beach near her home. "Both are really intense and really important."

Many of her colleagues on Vancouver Island agree.

Off the west coast of Canada, Vancouver Island has been ground zero for assisted suicide in the country. It was here that Sue Rodriguez, a 42-year-old suffering from amyotrophic lateral sclerosis, or A.L.S., began her battle to die with dignity in the 1990s, going all the way to the Supreme Court. "If I cannot give consent to my own death, whose body is this? Who owns my life?" she famously said.

The court sided against her in 1993, ruling that the state's interest was protecting life's sanctity. Less than five months later, Ms. Rodriguez died in the company of a friend, from what the police called a "doctor-assisted suicide" — although they never pressed charges. Seventeen years later, other patients and lawyers in British Columbia picked up Ms. Rodriguez's case. This time, the Supreme Court struck down the criminal sanctions against medical professionals who assist in suicide and perform euthanasia in prescribed circumstances.

Under the new regulations passed by the government, participants must be adults who are in an advanced state of a "grievous and irremediable medical condition." Their suffering must be intolerable and their natural death "reasonably foreseeable" — meaning people with long-term disabilities are not eligible unless they are near death. Patients must also be deemed mentally capable of consenting to the procedure moments before it happens. This stipulation is among the most debated parts of the law since it automatically bars people with dementia, even if they give advance consent.

Unlike in American states where similar laws exist, the Canadian system puts doctors and nurse practitioners at its center. They must not only determine whether a patient is eligible, but also oversee administration of the lethal medication. Doctors are not legally bound to participate, but in most provinces are expected to refer patients to colleagues who do.

Many doctors have refused to take part, believing that the law goes against their Hippocratic oath. Christian doctors in Ontario are taking their professional college to court, arguing that the requirement to directly refer patients infringes on their religious freedoms. On the other side, the lawyers who won the Supreme Court case have filed suit on behalf of people suffering intolerably from illnesses that are not terminal. They think the law should be expanded.

The public backlash many doctors feared against the law never materialized. Still, most doctors across Canada who have chosen to participate have done so quietly, even asking patients to withhold their names from their obituaries.

The exception has been on Vancouver Island, where Dr. Green and many of her colleagues advertise the service and publish their email addresses and phone numbers online. They have formed a national organization on medically assisted suicide and are holding their first conference in June.

The area of Victoria where Mr. Shields lived. He was fond of the wild and rugged landscapes of British Columbia.

And residents here have embraced it like nowhere else. With a population of just 771,000, Vancouver Island is the country's retirement community as well as a hotbed for alternative lifestyles. Of the 803 people across the country who chose medical deaths in the first six months since the law passed, 80 of them were from here.

Dr. Green and her colleagues have witnessed how the law is changing not only the method of dying, but also the rituals around it. Many patients are planning goodbye parties, requesting special last meals and choosing to die at home.

"You don't judge a civilization by its riches, but by how it treats its vulnerable," Dr. Green said. "I think this is a mark of our humanity."

She's never understood doctors who say offering lethal medicine goes against their training. "I think people go into medicine because they want to help people," she said. "This is on the continuum of care of helping people."

She and other doctors said that most of their patients suffer more from psychological than physical pain. Just being approved for a medical death can be therapeutic. For some, the knowledge that they can control their exit translates into more peaceful final days.

The first death Dr. Green oversaw remains her touchstone. The man was dying from liver failure and his family opened their home for friends and neighbors to drop in and say goodbye. When he died, they all held him, including Dr. Green.

"It was a beautiful event," she said. "It felt really like we were giving him a gift. It felt so good."

Last October, Dr. Green participated in a panel discussion about medical deaths in the little public recreation center near Mr. Shields's home. Sitting in the audience that day was Ms. Hood.

'I DON'T WANT TO SUFFER ANYMORE'

By the time Dr. Green paid her first house call to the couple's home three months later, Mr. Shields's neuropathy had progressed so much that his feet were permanently numb and covered in sores. He wore leather gloves on his hands, which had also lost all feeling. His skin was distressingly itchy. He could no longer swallow dry food. He vomited regularly.

When he noticed his wife and daughter were shielding their torment about his declining health, he asked them to start a new tradition. Every Wednesday, they would light the dining room candles, put out the nicest hand-thrown pottery and silverware, and share their grief, anxiety and anger with him. They also began to discuss the plans for his death. The result, he said, was that they felt closer.

"What could be more meaningful than planning for the end of your life?" he said.

He focused his energy on a workshop his wife helped facilitate called "Living Well, Dying Well," speaking openly about his pending death and making new, intimate friends. While many people approaching death become increasingly insular, Mr. Shields continued to expand his world.

Still, he had not set a death date. He expected to live through spring, and hoped to see summer blossoms emerge in his garden.

One night in February, less than two weeks after he was approved for assisted dying, Mr. Shields awoke in his favorite maroon chair in the living room in a delirious state. He had fallen asleep reading and missed a round of medication.

"He didn't make any sense," Ms. Hood said. "He was totally incoherent."

A nurse from the Victoria Hospice was dispatched to the house in the middle of the night. She thought he had an infection and put an intravenous catheter into his arm so his wife could administer medications.

In the morning, it took three women — his wife, his stepdaughter and a friend — an hour to guide him a dozen paces to the washroom. One lifted each foot with her hands. They realized that he had been in much more pain than he let on and that they could no longer care for him at home.

Later that morning, he was settled into a room in Victoria's only hospice, an Art Deco, cotton-candy pink building on the edge of a hospital. It opened in 1946 as a maternity ward and retains that ambience.

His family carted in pots of daffodils to scatter around his room, along with some of his favorite books and CDs. They loaded up the bar fridge with food and settled into the brown sofa chairs in the corner to wait and worry.

A testament to Mr. Shields's wide legacy: A nurse on the floor had been one of his foster care cases from his time as a social worker, and a counselor at the hospice was one of his oldest friends who had worked with him back in 1971.

Three days later, Dr. Green came to check in on Mr. Shields and tell him she was going on vacation with her husband. That put the family in a difficult position. If Mr. Shields wanted to proceed with his death, he had two options: schedule it for the very next day or in two weeks, on March 24.

"Can you imagine?" said Ms. Hood, sitting on a couch in the hospice's comfortable lounge. A half-finished puzzle had been left on a nearby table and a guitar hung on the wall for general use. Tears filled her blue eyes. "Your partner all of a sudden is going to die the next day. It's bad enough he's going to die in a few weeks. But tomorrow? That was too much."

The scheduling was not the only agonizing part of the decision. She also worried about Mr. Shields's mental capacity. He was not thinking clearly. That morning, he asked her if she had brought his sleeping bag. He was going on a voyage, he said.

She was not sure if his confusion stemmed from the disease's progression or the cocktail of pain medication hospice doctors had put him on. Either way, she worried that his lucidity would slip further and that Dr. Green would not be able to perform the procedure.

"John is right smack in the middle of the issue he was worried about — his ability to give consent," Ms. Hood said.

This is the fine edge patients must balance — stretching out the last moments of their lives before the option to control their deaths disappears. It is a bit like playing chicken.

Dr. Green has had to disqualify a number of patients who could no longer understand the gravity of the decision before them.

"It feels like there should be flexibility in the law, but right now there isn't," Dr. Green said. "Sometimes, it feels cruel."

Over the next few days, Mr. Shields's pain got worse and worse. None of the usual treatments worked. For the first time in their decade-long marriage, his wife saw him cry. He became weaker. He lost weight. And his mind continued to be murky. He could express his thoughts for a few sentences, then lose them in a rush of words.

The hospice's expertise was end-stage cancer, not amyloidosis. Mr. Shields's case was the first its medical chief of staff had seen in his 20 years of palliative care.

Two weeks after Mr. Shields was admitted, doctors tried lidocaine — a powerful local anesthetic commonly used by dentists. For

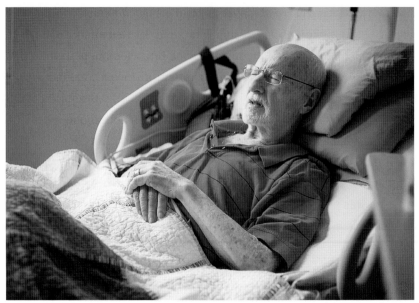

the first time in months, Mr. Shields slept through the night. His thoughts became noticeably clearer.

Once impossibly and improbably far away, March 24 barreled down like a speeding train. Family and friends who visited him at the hospice felt conflicted. They knew this was what he wanted, but it broke their hearts — particularly now that he seemed more like himself. One moment, his niece wanted to rip off the remaining time like a Band-Aid; the next, she longed to linger inside each precious second.

"This should be easier on me because it's predictable. But it isn't," said Donna Morton, who had lived in the family's spare bedroom for more than a year and considered Mr. Shields her spiritual father. "I feel a little panicky."

Buoyed by his improvement, his wife hoped he might push off the date. But he did not want to. "No matter how I looked at it, I saw pain," he said. "No matter how I looked at my life from this moment on, I see personal, physical unbearable suffering. I don't want to suffer anymore."

He also felt like a pioneer. Recently, he dreamed that he was sweeping up large shards of glass from a hallway, making it safe for others who would pass that way after him.

The idea for a final party with fixings from Swiss Chalet came to him because of the extraordinary kindness he had received at the hospice — from friends and strangers alike. That morning, a hospice volunteer gave him a pastel-colored homemade quilt, which was now covering his lap. He wanted to spread some of that "loving energy" around.

"Besides," he said, "I like chicken."

Ms. Hood felt like escaping to the woods to cry. It was her husband's last night, and he wanted to have a party with food from a restaurant they had never eaten at together. But this was one last token of love she could give him. Putting aside her anxiety and sorrow, she sent out an email invitation to select friends.

It was titled "John's Farewell Party."

SAYING GOODBYE. BUT FIRST, CHICKEN.

On March 23 at 6 p.m., a heavy atmosphere hung over the small hospice room aspirationally called a solarium.

No one knew what to expect from a living wake, not even Penny Allport, the life-cycle celebrant Mr. Shields had asked to help guide the party and preside over his death the next morning. She was trained and certified for funerals and weddings, but nothing like this.

Efforts had been made to convert what normally felt like a doctor's waiting room into a place worthy of the occasion. A pale green hospice blanket served as a tablecloth over two adjacent coffee tables, which were decorated with a vase of simple daisies and daffodils and strewn with cue cards, each of which bore one of Mr. Shields's favorite quotations in colored ink.

"Tell me, what is it you plan to do with your one wild and precious life?"
— Mary Oliver

"There is nothing more mysterious than destiny — of a person, of our species, of our planet, or of the universe itself." — Brian Swimme

A small electronic keyboard was tucked into a corner and repurposed as a bar. On one end were bottles of a local Shiraz with "Rebellion: On Your Own Terms" on the label. On the other was a chocolate hazelnut cake Mr. Shields had requested. It came from a virtuous bakery, even by Victoria's hippie standards — grain bought locally and ground in-house. The foil to Swiss Chalet, it captured the opposite extremes of Mr. Shields's personality.

People milled about in a nearby kitchen area, taming their grief and nerves by pouring out bowls of nuts and chopping apples. More arrived, bearing instruments and flowers.

At 6:12, two nurses wearing blue latex gloves wheeled Mr. Shields into the solarium and plugged his medication pump into a wall socket. He was sitting up in his giant humming airbed, a royal purple shawl hanging around his neck like a towel after a tennis game.

It was as if a switch had been flipped. With his appearance, the room's heaviness lifted.

"You think I'm only going to have one portion?" Mr. Shields said when presented with his plate of Swiss Chalet chicken. Laughter erupted around him.

His stepdaughter, Ms. Sanchez, pulled his favorite black-brimmed skipper's hat down over his brow.

Once he finished his meal, Ms. Allport began the farewell ceremony. Tall with long, wavy brown hair streaked with gray, she had the posture of a yoga instructor, which she had been for years. Standing behind him, she held up a white khata — a Buddhist prayer scarf — and instructed each guest to place a verbal blessing in it for Mr. Shields. She called his death his "great blooming."

"My name is Penny," she said, pressing the scarf to her chest. "I offer the blessing of courageous heart."

The scarf was passed to Ms. Hood, who held her husband's hand and looked into his eyes as she spoke.

"My name is Robin," she said, her soft voice catching in emotion. "I bring the blessing of community, of justice, of peace and of having been the partner of a wise and beautiful loving man."

The room was filled to capacity. Two dozen people hovered over Mr. Shields, pressing themselves against the walls and folding their bodies onto the floor. Others bunched by the door.

Dale Perkins, a retired United Church minister and a member of the men's spiritual circle led by Mr. Shields, hung over the foot of his bed like a mesmerized child.

The scarf traveled reverently from hand to hand. Ears strained to catch each word.

"My name is Sarah," said a dark-haired woman with a deep voice, seated in a chair in the corner. "And I love you."

A box of Kleenex was passed like a busker's hat at a variety show. Mr. Perkins pulled a handkerchief from his pocket and mopped his face.

One after another, proclamations of love, admiration and gratitude poured forth. They thanked their host for opening his door when they were brokenhearted. They thanked him for his friendship. They thanked him for his courage.

"I thank you for the gift you are giving us tonight," said Heather Fox, the grief counselor he met in 1971.

Time and again, Mr. Shields acknowledged and thanked each speaker and doled out some tailor-made insight or joke to lighten the mood. When a former colleague planted a goodbye kiss on his lips, he unleashed more laughter with the quip: "I was just thinking, 'I'd like to see more of that.' Then I thought, 'That's not a good idea.' "

Ms. Hood saw the priest her husband once was, offering blessings and benedictions to his congregation. Union friends remembered his speaking before giant crowds at rallies in the 1980s. "He has never met an audience he didn't love," said Preben Skovgaard, his former chief of staff and best friend.

Mr. Skovgaard found the public weight of the moment too much and escaped to the hall for most of the evening. When he was finally yanked by one arm into the room, he offered a loving roast.

"You've talked a lot about some of John's abilities," he said. "I want to talk about one more. And that is, he has an innate ability to piss you off."

This was an Irish wake, without grief's frantic edge. Mr. Shields was still here, sipping his final glass of American beer. Many looked over at him with wonder, understanding that he was offering them one final lesson.

As the party wound down, Ms. Fox handed out the lyrics to the Celtic folk song "The Parting Glass." They serenaded him.

But since it falls, unto my lot,
That I should rise and you should not,
I'll gently rise and I'll softly call,
Good night and joy be with you all.

Mr. Shields was waning. He had already tried to make a speech, but his mind wandered off script. This time, he hoped to get through what he called the "verses of a special departure song." He closed his eyes. Eighteen seconds passed, until it seemed perhaps he had drifted off to sleep.

"When we blossom forth into the night," he said finally, his eyes still closed, "what do we hear? We hear the silence of the bees. We hear the brushing of the wind in the trees. We hear the whisper of wind to branch and branch to wind. And we know that we are close to the end of the journey."

He opened his eyes. "And to all of us, who have come together. You are seeing me get sad. It would never happen without some sadness."

He thanked his friends, one more time. When they came to their death and they heard the song of the bees, he hoped they were as happy as he was. "I'm welcoming you all to sing it with joy," he said.

At 7:40, the nurses arrived and unplugged his medication pump. Mr. Shields waved to his friends as his bed was wheeled out of the solarium. "I will see you later," he said, smiling.

'WHO COULD ASK FOR ANYTHING MORE?'

The morning of Mr. Shields's death, Dr. Green took Benji for a walk on the beach before driving to the hospital pharmacy to pick up the drugs for the procedure.

Patients have two options: They can drink a cocktail of lethal medication, or they can have the doctor administer drugs intravenously. Like nearly everyone, Mr. Shields chose the second.

The pharmacist had already prepared the doses for Dr. Green. There were four drugs, drawn up into syringes. First, an anti-anxiety medication called midazolam that puts most people to sleep quickly. Then a small amount of lidocaine to numb the vein, followed by a large dose of propofol — the anesthetic often used to ease people to sleep before operations. The thick, white fluid filled two fat syringes the diameter of quarters. Dr. Green always warned family and friends about the ominous size of those needles before she started the procedure, so they were not frightened.

The propofol would put Mr. Shields into a coma. The final drug she would inject into his IV catheter was a paralyzer called rocuronium. It stops all movement.

Dr. Green would administer doses of saline after all but one of these drugs, to make sure they completely entered Mr. Shields's system.

The pharmacist gave Dr. Green a second dosage of everything, in case she needed to restart the protocol. That has happened to her only once. It involved a younger patient, whose heart took 19 minutes to stop — nine long minutes more than average. Since then, Dr. Green has set a limit. If a patient's heart does not stop 15 minutes after she administers the propofol, she starts the entire procedure again, just to be sure.

The pharmacist packed the medication into two blue boxes, like the ones construction workers use to carry their lunches. Dr. Green took one in each hand.

Another doctor on Vancouver Island admits she has trouble sleeping the night before a procedure. One other has her partner drive her home afterward — she is so emotionally drained.

Dr. Green has neither of those problems. She was well rested and happy heading to the hospice that morning. If she felt jittery, it was only because she was double- and triple-checking the procedure in her mind and making sure she was ready.

She took the elevator to the third floor and walked down the hospice's beige hall to Mr. Shields's room. They talked intimately for a few minutes. She asked him if he still wanted to go ahead. He did.

She was convinced that he was of sound enough mind to make this decision. He signed the last page of official paperwork, confirming that he had been given the chance to change his mind and that he still wanted to go through with this.

Dr. Green instructed a nurse to set up his intravenous line while she slipped down the hall to go over the procedure with his friends and family.

She assured them that his death would be peaceful. He would simply go into a deep sleep and might even snore. But, if at any time it got too hard, they should leave the room. "There are no medals for staying," she said. "There's no judgment for leaving."

Mr. Shields had asked five people to be there: his wife, his stepdaughter, Mr. Skovgaard, Ms. Fox and Ms. Allport, who was overseeing his death ceremony. When they entered his room, Mr. Shields greeted them with a smile. His blue eyes twinkled, matching a fresh aqua T-shirt. The quilt of unexpected kindness was spread over his legs.

The room was dark and cool. The overhead lights were off and one of the windows was open. Across its sill, an altar had been fashioned with cedar boughs, smooth stones, eagle feathers, a small red candle and a tiny bell. The emerald moss coating the limbs of a giant Garry oak tree outside glowed into the room.

Since Mr. Shields could not die in his garden, his garden had been brought to him.

A large white candle flickered on the night stand beside him. The hospital tray that had held his meals for the past two weeks was pushed to the side. Upon it was one of Dr. Green's blue boxes, and eight syringes lined up neatly in a row.

The group formed a circle around Mr. Shields, with his wife at his head, touching his shoulder. He asked her what was happening, and she recounted what Dr. Green had said about the procedure, adding that he should go toward the light.

"Sounds perfect," he said, giving a thumbs up.

It didn't sound so perfect to her, she replied. It was as good as it was going to get, he said.

Ms. Allport began the ceremony she had designed with input from Mr. Shields and inspirations from a mix of cultural traditions.

She opened her arms wide, turned to each direction of the room and related it to Mr. Shields's life. The east was the wind on which his beloved eagles fly. The south was fire and the snake shedding its skin, as he soon would. The west was water, filled with whales that passed his house. The north was the trees, like the thousands he had protected.

She had taken the bell from the windowsill and rang it between each turn, its tone bouncing lightly from the walls.

She called up to the sky and the heavens, and crouched down on the floor, thanking the earth for carrying his body for 78 years.

When she finished, she paused. There was not a sound in the room.

Mr. Shields, she said, would need ancestors to help guide his journey. They needed to be summoned. She asked everyone to mimic a movement she noticed Mr. Shields making recently: two hands placed on the heart and then swung open like saloon doors. If the names of ancestors came to their minds, they should call them out.

Ms. Hood whispered the names of his father, mother and former wife, Madeleine.

Mr. Shields opened his eyes and quietly said Rumi, the 13th-century Persian poet.

Ms. Sanchez held his right hand in hers, sobbing. Her nails were painted metal green, accentuating how pale his numb fingers had become. One of his regrets was that he could no longer feel a touch like this.

His wife leaned over and told him his love had been radiant. When she finished, he said, "Thank you, my darling."

Mr. Shields then began singing a refrain from an old Gershwin Broadway tune: "Who could ask for anything more?"

The others joined in. "I got daisies, in green pastures. I've got my man. Who could ask for anything more?"

The singing came like intermission during a heartbreaking movie. Mr. Shields was delighting in life, right to the end. The ritual held the moment's solemn structure; he was adding some human lightness. He did not seem afraid.

The day before, when Ms. Allport asked him if there was a poem he would like read, he asked for a Catholic one: The Prayer of St. Francis of Assisi.

Standing at his feet, Ms. Fox unfolded a copy. "Lord, make me an instrument of thy peace," she began. Mr. Shields mouthed the words silently. He had left Catholicism almost five decades before, but Catholicism had not entirely left him. It was as if all the disparate strands of his life were being woven into this final moment.

Where there is hatred, let me sow love;
Where there is injury, pardon;
Where there is doubt, faith;
Where there is despair, hope.

"I think I've learned that lesson," he said, when she finished.

For all of his openness and shared emotions, Mr. Shields was a stoic man. But when his wife told him that fires were burning for him on different islands, and that native elders were playing drums for him farther north on Vancouver Island, he closed his eyes and wept.

He talked about his father and his mother. In his life, he said, he had come to believe that everyone shared the same cosmic energy.

"We are all one," he said.

He thanked everyone for their kindness. The sound of cars passing in the street below echoed up faintly through the window. Hands touched shoulders and hands.

Dr. Green leaned over and quietly asked him if he was ready.

By then, Ms. Allport had laid the white khata from the night before across Mr. Shields's neck. His eyes were closed. He opened them and slowly scanned the faces around him, taking in each one.

"Are we ready, friends?" he asked. He turned his head to look at the doctor. "Yes, Stefanie," he said. "I am ready."

She took the first syringe from the table and screwed its tip into the IV catheter on the tender side of Mr. Shields's left arm, then pressed its plunger down.

He closed his eyes. His face relaxed. He appeared to go into a deep sleep.

The only sound in the room was his stepdaughter's crying.

One after the other, Dr. Green went through the syringes until none were left on the table. Mr. Shields's body remained still. He made no grimaces. The only change was a slight yellowing of his face.

Dr. Green pulled her stethoscope from around her neck and listened to his heart. It was still beating.

A few minutes later, she did it again. And then, a third time.

Finally, 13 minutes after she had administered the first medication, she nodded to Ms. Hood. Mr. Shields was gone.

GOING HOME TO HIS GARDEN

That evening, Mr. Shields's body lay on a stretcher in his backyard. A large purple sheet was draped over his face and body, followed by a thick brown blanket — as though he had been tucked into bed.

His favorite black hat with the skipper's brim had been pulled over his concealed brow, and a thin book of poetry slipped beneath his pillow: "The Subject Tonight Is Love" by Hafiz, a 14th-century Persian.

A beige canvas shelter protected him from the sprinkling rain. Boughs of cedar, white currant and flowering plum hung in bouquets from its corners, and its lip was decorated with prayer flags.

A candle flickered on a nearby table. Friends sat in chairs that were placed around him.

For Ms. Hood, the best part of this new way of dying in Canada was also the worst part. The scheduling tormented her and organized her. While her husband was intentional about his death, she was intentional about his final rites. They would be administered at home, by his loved ones, and not by the funeral industry.

She believed that her husband's spirit would stay with his body for two days before journeying on. So someone was always in the garden with him — reading poetry, recounting stories or just sitting silently, keeping him company until he was taken to the crematory.

Neighbors dropped off food, wine and cords of wood for the fire, which burned continuously. At night, Mr. Shields's friends stood around it and serenaded his still body and memory. It was spiritual and poignant, ritualistic and community-based.

"He would have loved it," his wife said.

Those two days, the weather was fickle — the rain gave way to sun, the wind to calm, and then it rained again. Flocks of birds arrived. Deer and raccoons visited.

The majestic Douglas firs swayed above Mr. Shields. His garden was wild and beautiful, just as he had loved it.

Produced by **GRAY BELTRAN**, **LESLYE DAVIS** and **ALEXANDRA GARCIA**.

Rules for Reporting a Planned Death: No Photos, No Pad, No Pen

BY CATHERINE PORTER | DEC. 18, 2017

Last March, as part of a series called The End, reported by Times correspondents around the world, John Shields of Victoria, British Columbia, permitted me to enter not just his life, but also his death. It was, undoubtedly, one of the most profound workdays I have ever had.

In May, I wrote this behind-the-scenes story about how I came to be in Mr. Shields's hospice room that morning. It was slated to be published at the same time as my story about his death, together with Leslye Davis's wonderful photos and video. But as often happens in journalism, it was held. Until now.

What I wrote then remains true today. I carry the memory of Mr. Shields's death with me like prayer beads. For me, it has become a mantra not only about dying well, but also about living well.

TORONTO — The first living wake I heard about was Rob Gray's.

His wife described how two dozen loved ones had gathered around him in his hospital bed a couple of hours before his scheduled death. They serenaded him, drank champagne and each delivered a loving tribute.

She called it an "end of life celebration."

I had been researching Medical Assistance in Dying (MAID), the neutral Canadian term for both assisted suicide and voluntary euthanasia by doctors and nurse practitioners. The government legalized it in June 2016 as the public debate pitting medical workers' rights against those of patients was raging in the country, as it still is.

More recently, I had begun to clip mentions of it from the obituaries. How was this new form of dying changing the rituals around death, I wondered.

Think about it: If you knew you were going to die tomorrow at 9 a.m., what would you do tonight? What would your family and friends do?

After hearing a dozen more stories like Mr. Gray's, I realized the country was quietly undergoing a profound cultural shift. Urged by my editor, Michael Slackman, I set out to document it intimately. But how would I find people who were sick enough to qualify for a medical death and would be willing to let a journalist poke around in what remained of their lives?

I decided to fly across Canada from Toronto — where I work as The New York Times's bureau chief — to Victoria, because doctors there were uncharacteristically open about providing this service. Seven agreed to pass on my request to their patients.

John Shields was the first patient I met. Together with my colleague Leslye Davis, we had tea in his kitchen and watched the doctor sign the forms qualifying him for a medical death.

He agreed to let us follow his story, but cautioned that he'd live through spring — summer even — so he doubted he'd make a good subject for us.

We met three other patients on that trip. One was a 92-year-old World War II veteran who had booked his death and then, overjoyed by his children's arrival for his goodbye party, postponed it. A couple of days later he told me he had changed his mind about our interview — his children were too upset.

I realized I needed to follow more than one person. I ended up shadowing three: Mr. Shields and two women, one in Toronto and one in Victoria.

In all three cases we struck a deal. They would welcome me into their private lives and thoughts at the ends of their lives but were free to tell me to buzz off at any time. The flip side? I might not write their stories.

One of those two women was June Vaile, a funny and forthright 80-year-old who was happy to die from cancer since macular degeneration had stolen her life's pleasures. Two days before her scheduled death she hugged me goodbye.

The second, a quiet, reflective woman named Eve McLeod, died from pancreatic cancer this past Tuesday morning. Even though she was approved for a medical death, she chose to die naturally in the end.

I flew back to Victoria when Mr. Shields was admitted to hospice and spent two days interviewing him in ten-minute bursts, between his two-hour naps. The pressure was enormous — to ask only the best, most insightful questions, and not soak up all his precious energy and remaining time. His wife, stepdaughter and an ever-growing line of friends bunched in the hospice lounge waiting their turns.

He was so weak and confused I thought he'd die before his scheduled death.

But he didn't. What's more, he decided he wanted a party, much like Mr. Gray's.

I was invited to attend both his last-night festivities and his death. While we were free to record his final party, the celebrant he'd chosen to oversee both ceremonies laid out some non-negotiable rules for his death. She believed Mr. Shields's spirit would be beginning a journey and all attention needed to support him. A detached witness would distract from that, she said. If I came, I had to participate. No photos, no recordings, no notepad.

As a journalist, being without a pen and paper on the job feels like being naked. But once I stepped into the room, I realized that vulnerability was important. Without the shield of my notepad, I could feel and respond to what is essentially one of life's most profound moments. I held hands with one of Mr. Shields's best friends. When it was over, I burst from the room in tears and unloaded everything I had experienced into Leslye's digital recorder. That same day, I checked my memories of the occasion with three other people who had been there to ensure they were accurate.

I've thought about Mr. Shields's death continually since then. I hope everyone I love dies with such peace. I am still astounded by his generosity that morning. I wonder if I will have his courage to beckon death rather than fight its arrival. I am not sure.

I know this: Mr. Shields was wrong about not being the right subject for this story. He was the perfect one.

Glossary

ALS Also known as Lou Gehrig's disease, an incurable disease that affects the neuromuscular system, weakening the muscles and impacting physical function. ALS is ultimately fatal.

arbiter A person who settles a dispute or has authority in a matter; a person who influences social behavior.

assisted suicide The suicide of a person with the assistance of another person, particularly a physician.

barbiturate A drug that acts as a nervous system depressant, creating a sedative and a sleep-inducing result. Can be fatal in dose.

bioethics The study of ethical issues and implications deriving from biological and medical research.

Death With Dignity Act A 1997 act passed by Oregon allowing terminally ill patients to end their lives through the voluntary self-administration of lethal medications prescribed by a physician.

dementia A decline in mental ability caused by brain injury, illness, or other factors.

eugenic sterilization Surgery removing the ability of an individual to produce offspring given to a person who is either mentally ill or mentally defective and will either severely handicap any future offspring through heredity or is unable to properly care for a child.

euthanasia The act or practice of killing or permitting the death of hopelessly sick or injured individuals in a relatively painless way for reasons of mercy.

geriatrics The branch of medicine dealing with the treatment of and care for elderly individuals.

Hippocratic oath An oath historically taken by physicians requiring them to uphold certain ethical standards.

hospice care An approach to care designed to give supportive care to people in the final phase of a terminal illness and focus on comfort and quality of life, rather than cure.

ignominious Behavior deserving or causing public disgrace or shame, dishonorable.

Not Dead Yet A national grassroots disability rights group that opposes the legalization of assisted suicide.

opiate A drug derived from opium that can induce sleep and alleviate pain. Opiates can be fatal in certain doses.

palliative care An approach to medical and nursing care focused on increasing quality of life and providing relief from the symptoms, pain, physical stress, and mental stress at any stage of illness.

Parkinson's Disease An incurable progressive nervous system disease that affects movement and in its latest stages can prove to be fatal.

physician-assisted suicide A physician facilitates a patient's death by providing the necessary means and/or information to enable the patient to perform the life-ending act.

taboo A social custom prohibiting or forbidding the carrying out or discussion of a particular practice or forbidding association with a particular person, place, or thing.

terminal illness An illness that is incurable and cannot be adequately treated. It can be reasonably expected that a terminal illness will result in the death of the patient.

Media Literacy Terms

"Media literacy" refers to the ability to access, understand, critically assess and create media. The following terms are important components of media literacy, and they will help you critically engage with the articles in this title.

angle The aspect of a news story that a journalist focuses on and develops.

attribution The method by which a source is identified or by which facts and information are assigned to the person who provided them.

balance Principle of journalism that both perspectives of an argument should be presented in a fair way.

bias A disposition of prejudice in favor of a certain idea, person or perspective.

caption Identifying copy for a picture; also called a legend or cutline.

column A type of story that is a regular feature, often on a recurring topic, written by the same journalist, generally known as a columnist.

commentary A type of story that is an expression of opinion on recent events by a journalist generally known as a commentator.

credibility The quality of being trustworthy and believable, said of a journalistic source.

editorial Article of opinion or interpretation.

human interest story A type of story that focuses on individuals and how events or issues affect their life, generally offering a sense of relatability to the reader.

impartiality Principle of journalism that a story should not reflect a journalist's bias and should contain balance.

intention The motive or reason behind something, such as the publication of a news story.

motive The reason behind something, such as the publication of a news story or a source's perspective on an issue.

news story An article or style of expository writing that reports news, generally in a straightforward fashion and without editorial comment.

op-ed An opinion piece that reflects a prominent individual's opinion on a topic of interest.

paraphrase The summary of an individual's words, with attribution, rather than a direct quotation of their exact words.

plagiarism An attempt to pass another person's work as one's own without attribution.

quotation The use of an individual's exact words indicated by the use of quotation marks and proper attribution.

reliability The quality of being dependable and accurate, said of a journalistic source.

rhetorical device Technique in writing intending to persuade the reader or communicate a message from a certain perspective.

source The origin of the information reported in journalism.

style A distinctive use of language in writing or speech; also a news or publishing organization's rules for consistent use of language with regards to spelling, punctuation, typography and capitalization, usually regimented by a house style guide.

tone A manner of expression in writing or speech.

Media Literacy Questions

1. Identify the various sources cited in the article " 'Aid in Dying' Movement Takes Hold in Some States" (on page 70). How does Erik Eckholm attribute information to each of these sources in his article? How effective are Eckholm's attributions in helping the reader identify his sources?

2. In "Push for the Right to Die Grows in the Netherlands" (on page 159), David Jolly paraphrases information from and directly quotes Dr. Petra de Jong. What are the strengths of the use of a paraphrase as opposed to a direct quote? What are the weaknesses?

3. Compare the headlines of "Fatal Mercies" (on page 10) and "On Assisted Suicide, Going Beyond 'Do No Harm' " (on page 29). Which is a more compelling headline, and why? How could the less compelling headline be changed to better draw the reader's interest?

4. What type of story is "Brittany Maynard, 'Death With Dignity' Ally, Dies at 29" (on page 139)? Can you identify another article in this collection that is the same type of story? What elements helped you come to your conclusion?

5. The article "Let Dying People End Their Suffering" (on page 44) is an example of an op-ed. Identify how Diane Rehm's attitude and tone help convey her opinion on the topic.

6. Does "Who May Die? California Patients and Doctors Wrestle With Assisted Suicide" (on page 88) use multiple sources? What are the strengths of using multiple sources in a journalistic piece? What are the weaknesses of relying heavily on only one or a few sources?

7. What is the intention of the article "At His Own Wake, Celebrating Life and the Gift of Death" (on page 185)? How effectively does it achieve its intended purpose?

8. Analyze the authors' reporting in "Lawsuit Seeks to Legalize Doctor-Assisted Suicide for Terminally Ill Patients in New York" (on page 81) and "Justin Trudeau Seeks to Legalize Assisted Suicide in Canada" (on page 170). Do you think one journalist is more impartial in their reporting than the other? If so, why do you think so?

9. Often, as a news story develops, a journalist's attitude toward the subject may change. Compare "Physician Aid in Dying Gains Acceptance in the U.S." (on page 98) and "A Debate Over 'Rational Suicide.' " (on page 50), both by Paula Span. Did new information discovered between the publication of these two articles change Span's perspective?

10. Identify each of the sources in "In Ill Doctor, a Surprise Reflection of Who Picks Assisted Suicide" (on page 114) as a primary source or a secondary source. Evaluate the reliability and credibility of each source. How does your evaluation of each source change your perspective on this article?

Citations

All citations in this list are formatted according to the
Modern Language Association's (MLA) style guide.

BOOK CITATION

THE NEW YORK TIMES EDITORIAL STAFF. *Assisted Suicide: Is It Right to Have the Choice?* New York: New York Times Educational Publishing, 2020.

ONLINE ARTICLE CITATIONS

ALTMAN, ANN M. "Casualties of War." *The New York Times*, 7 Nov. 2015, opinionator.blogs.nytimes.com/2015/11/07/casualties-of-war/.

ARONSON, LOUISE. "Weighing the End of Life." *The New York Times*, 2 Feb. 2013, www.nytimes.com/2013/02/03/opinion/sunday/weighing -the-end-of-life.html.

AUSTEN, IAN. "Justin Trudeau Seeks to Legalize Assisted Suicide in Canada." *The New York Times*, 14 Apr. 2016, www.nytimes.com/2016/04/15/world /americas/canadian-prime-minister-seeks-to-legalize-physician -assistedsuicide.html.

BILEFSKY, DAN, AND CHRISTOPHER F. SCHUETZE. "Dutch Law Would Allow Assisted Suicide for Healthy Older People." *The New York Times*, 13 Oct. 2016, https://www.nytimes.com/2016/10/14/world/europe/dutch-law -would-allow-euthanasia-for-healthy-elderly-people.html.

BLINDER, ALAN. "Doctor Loses License Over Assisted Suicides." *The New York Times*, 30 Dec. 2014, www.nytimes.com/2014/12/31/us/doctor-loses -license-over-assisted-suicides.html.

BROWN, ROBBIE. "Arrests Draw New Attention to Assisted Suicide." *The New York Times*, 10 Mar. 2009, www.nytimes.com/2009/03/11/us/11suicide.html.

BRUNI, FRANK. "Fatal Mercies." *The New York Times*, 10 Aug. 2013, www .nytimes.com/2013/08/11/opinion/sunday/bruni-fatal-mercies.html.

BURNS, JOHN F. "With Help, Conductor and Wife Ended Lives." *The New York*

Times, 14 July 2009, www.nytimes.com/2009/07/15/world/europe/15britain
.html.

CAREY, BENEDICT. "Assisted Suicide Study Questions Its Use for Mentally Ill."
The New York Times, 10 Feb. 2016, www.nytimes.com/2016/02/11/health
/assisted-suicide-mental-disorders.html.

DOUTHAT, ROSS. "The Last Right." *The New York Times*, 11 Oct. 2014, www
.nytimes.com/2014/10/12/opinion/sunday/ross-douthat-why-america-is
-moving-slowly-on-assisted-suicide.html.

ECKHOLM, ERIK. " 'Aid in Dying' Movement Takes Hold in Some States."
The New York Times, 7 Feb. 2014, www.nytimes.com/2014/02/08/us
/easing-terminal-patients-path-to-death-legally.html.

FISHER, IAN. "A Poet Crusades for the Right to Die His Way." *The New York
Times*, 20 Dec. 2006, www.nytimes.com/2006/12/20/world/europe/20welby
.html.

GOLDMAN, BOB. "For Those at Death's Door, a Case for 'Life Panels.' " *The New
York Times*, 19 Nov. 2013, www.nytimes.com/2013/11/20/your-money
/for-those-at-deaths-door-a-case-for-life-panels.html.

HABERMAN, CLYDE. "Stigma Around Physician-Assisted Dying Lingers."
The New York Times, 22 Mar. 2015, www.nytimes.com/2015/03/23/us
/stigma-around-physician-assisted-dying-lingers.html.

HAFNER, KATIE. "In Ill Doctor, a Surprise Reflection of Who Picks Assisted
Suicide." *The New York Times*, 11 Aug. 2012, www.nytimes.com/2012/08/12
/health/policy/in-ill-doctor-a-surprise-reflection-of-who-picks-assisted
-suicide.html.

HARTOCOLLIS, ANEMONA. "Lawsuit Seeks to Legalize Doctor-Assisted Suicide
for Terminally Ill Patients in New York." *The New York Times*, 3 Feb. 2015,
www.nytimes.com/2015/02/04/nyregion/lawsuit-seeks-to-legalize-doctor
-assisted-suicide-for-terminally-ill-patients-in-new-york.html.

HENIG, ROBIN MARANTZ. "A Life-or-Death Situation." *The New York Times*,
17 July 2013, www.nytimes.com/2013/07/21/magazine/a-life-or-death
-situation.html.

JOLLY, DAVID. "Push for the Right to Die Grows in the Netherlands." *The New
York Times*, 2 Apr. 2012, www.nytimes.com/2012/04/03/health/push-for
-the-right-to-die-grows-in-the-netherlands.html.

JOSEPH, YONETTE. "Why David Goodall, 104, Renowned Australian Scientist,
Wants to Die." *The New York Times*, 3 May 2018, www.nytimes.com/2018/05
/03/world/australia/david-goodall-right-to-die.html.

JOSEPH, YONETTE, AND ILIANA MAGRA. "David Goodall, 104, Scientist Who Fought to Die on His Terms, Ends His Life." *The New York Times*, 10 May 2018, www.nytimes.com/2018/05/10/world/europe/david-goodall-australia -scientist-dead.html.

LANDLER, MARK. "Assisted Suicide of Healthy 79-Year-Old Renews German Debate on Right to Die." *The New York Times*, 3 July 2008, www.nytimes .com/2008/07/03/world/europe/03germany.html.

LERNER, BARRON H. "The Death of the Doctor's Dog." *The New York Times*, 6 Feb. 2018, www.nytimes.com/2018/02/06/well/live/death-dying-doctors -dog-euthanasia.html.

LOVETT, IAN, AND RICHARD PÉREZ-PEÑA. "California Governor Signs Assisted Suicide Bill Into Law." *The New York Times*, 5 Oct. 2015, www.nytimes .com/2015/10/06/us/california-governor-signs-assisted-suicide-bill-into -law.html.

LYALL, SARAH. "The Last Thing Mom Asked." *The New York Times*, 31 Aug. 2018, www.nytimes.com/2018/08/31/sunday-review/mother-death -euthanasia.html.

MALIK, KENAN. "Charlie Gard and Our Moral Confusion." *The New York Times*, 19 July 2017, www.nytimes.com/2017/07/19/opinion/charlie-gard-and-our -moral-confusion.html.

MATTLIN, BEN. "Suicide by Choice? Not So Fast." *The New York Times*, 31 Oct. 2012, www.nytimes.com/2012/11/01/opinion/suicide-by-choice-not-so-fast .html.

MEDINA, JENNIFER. "Who May Die? California Patients and Doctors Wrestle With Assisted Suicide." *The New York Times*, 9 June 2016, www.nytimes .com/2016/06/10/us/assisted-suicide-california-patients-and-doctors.html.

PORTER, CATHERINE. "At His Own Wake, Celebrating Life and the Gift of Death." *The New York Times*, 25 May 2017, www.nytimes.com/2017/05/25 /world/canada/euthanasia-bill-john-shields-death.html.

PORTER, CATHERINE. "Rules for Reporting a Planned Death: No Photos, No Pad, No Pen." *The New York Times*, 18 Dec. 2017, www.nytimes.com/2017 /12/18/insider/rules-for-reporting-a-planned-death-john-shields-canada .html.

POVOLEDO, ELISABETTA. "Italy to Allow Living Wills and the Refusal of End-of-Life Care." *The New York Times*, 14 Dec. 2017, www.nytimes.com/2017/12/14 /world/europe/italy-living-will-end-of-life-right-to-die-assisted-suicide .html.

REHM, DIANE. "Let Dying People End Their Suffering." *The New York Times,* 7 June 2018, www.nytimes.com/2018/06/07/opinion/california-end-of-life -aid-in-dying.html.

ROJAS, RICK. "Was a Scientist's Death Murder or an 'Act of Mercy'?" *The New York Times,* 28 Aug. 2018, www.nytimes.com/2018/08/28/world/australia /euthanasia-mary-white.html.

SAYARE, SCOTT. "French Families Challenge Doctors on Wrenching End-of-Life Decisions." *The New York Times,* 31 July 2014, www.nytimes.com/2014 /08/01/world/europe/french-families-challenge-doctors-on-wrenching -end-of-life-decisions-medicalized-hospital-deaths.html.

SCHWARTZ, JOHN. "A Polarizing Figure in End-of-Life Debates." *The New York Times,* 4 June 2011, www.nytimes.com/2011/06/05/us/05suicide.html.

SCHWARTZ, JOHN, AND JAMES ESTRIN. "In Oregon, Choosing Death Over Suffering." *The New York Times,* 1 June 2004, https://www.nytimes.com/2004 /06/01/science/in-oregon-choosing-death-over-suffering.html.

SLOTNICK, DANIEL E. "Brittany Maynard, 'Death With Dignity' Ally, Dies at 29." *The New York Times,* 3 Nov. 2014, www.nytimes.com/2014/11/04/us /brittany-maynard-death-with-dignity-ally-dies-at-29.html.

SPAN, PAULA. "A Debate Over 'Rational Suicide.' " *The New York Times,* 31 Aug. 2018, www.nytimes.com/2018/08/31/health/suicide-elderly.html.

SPAN, PAULA. "Gorsuch Staunchly Opposes 'Aid in Dying.' Does It Matter?" *The New York Times,* 24 Feb. 2017, www.nytimes.com/2017/02/24/health /neil-gorsuch-aid-in-dying-supreme-court.html.

SPAN, PAULA. "Physician Aid in Dying Gains Acceptance in the U.S." *The New York Times,* 16 Jan. 2017, www.nytimes.com/2017/01/16/health /physician-aid-in-dying.html.

WARRAICH, HAIDER JAVED. "On Assisted Suicide, Going Beyond 'Do No Harm.' " *The New York Times,* 4 Nov. 2016, www.nytimes.com/2016/11 /05/opinion/on-assisted-suicide-going-beyond-do-no-harm.html.

ZITTER, JESSICA NUTIK. "Should I Help My Patients Die?" *The New York Times,* 5 Aug. 2017, www.nytimes.com/2017/08/05/opinion/sunday /dying-doctors-palliative-medicine.html.

Index

This book is current up until the time of printing. For the most up-to-date reporting, visit www.nytimes.com.